CW00549316

Forty Seven

by Jeremy Ford

ISBN 978-0-9574330-0-7
£75.00

First published in the United Kingdom in 2012
by Restaurant Associates.

Restaurant Associates
24 Martin Lane
London EC4R ODR

+44 (0)20 7280 0700
info@restaurantassocaiets.co.uk
www.restaurantassociates.co.uk

Contents

Foreword

I believe that there are few things in life that can bring people together as powerfully as great food. More than that, every day I see how eating well can help people at work perform at their very best.

The Culinary team at Restaurant Associates led by our Culinary Director Jeremy Ford (whose book this is) — create inspirational food for our Clients, their guests and their employees. I wanted to give Jeremy and his brilliant team a way to share both what motivates them to create such outstanding food and a chance to show everyone how beautiful the outcome can be.

Moments of culinary inspiration and creativity at Restaurant Associates don't just shine brightly and then disappear into the ether — instead we catch them in our cloud. That way, every brilliant innovation is captured for us all to use — every day. Art and science coming together - smart stuff indeed!

The inspiration behind this book has come from our talented people, skilled and creative chefs including our associate chefs Albert Roux OBE, Michel Roux Jr, Gary Rhodes OBE and Jason Atherton. We're also highlighting our rising stars right alongside the Michelin star chefs in recognition of their outstanding talent and to evidence the incredible skill, passion and commitment that they bring to us and our clients each and every day. We are so proud of both them and what we do!

Good food brings people together all around the world. The experience and memory of sharing a meal around a table with family and friends is one of life's great pleasures. Why should our places of work be any different? .... We believe it shouldn't; turn the pages and see if you agree ?

I'm sure that once you've enjoyed just one of these dishes you'll see why I think that leading this brilliant team is the best job in London — and why I absolutely love it!

Enjoy.

Andy Harris
Managing Director
Restaurant Associates

For me, food is at the very heart of so much in life. It's my job, but it's also my passion. I love cooking almost as much as I love eating.

I'm extremely lucky to have one of the best chef jobs in the industry. It's taken me to many amazing places and restaurants. That includes my favourite city - New York.

I'm inspired by the constantly evolving food scene, and by the chefs at the very top of our industry who never stop pushing the boundaries. Our great chefs within Restaurant Associates inspire me too. Their drive, passion and constant thirst for knowledge and skill keep me going. I'm also inspired by food producers. A simple visit to a farm or a market can be a great tonic. All of which is fantastic. But I'm still never happier than when I'm just cooking.

Like most other chefs, the thing that drives me is bringing pleasure to people. It's that simple. Recognition for cooking good food is what all chefs crave. For that reason, I've dreamt of publishing a book for a long time, to showcase our talented chefs. I collect the latest cook books based on temples of gastronomy from around the world. Whilst being inspired by them, I've always felt that the food from many of our chefs, is just as impressive. So it has been a real pleasure to create this book. It's also started a real buzz within my whole team and I hope it continues to inspire them to keep our food at the cutting edge.

Actually, the hardest part was deciding which chefs to include. Here you'll find just eleven of our team and four of our associate chefs. There are so many others that cook to the same high standard that the book could have had three times as many pages - with great dishes from them all.

Why 47? It's the number of dishes in this book. It didn't need a fancy title or an elaborate cover. I love the fact that we've kept it so simple.

I wanted to show each chef's individual style. So the book focuses on fine dining and casual dining dishes. But this is only a small part of what we do. Every day, our chefs are creating fantastic and creative canapés, buffets, salad bars and working lunches. Even the humble sandwich is important. It makes no difference to us, whether we're dreaming up a six course tasting menu in a private dining room or serving breakfast in a food court.

I'm incredibly proud to be introducing this book and also sharing a few of my own recipes alongside those from talented chefs.

Jeremy Ford

Jeremy Ford
Culinary Director
Restaurant Associates

Loch Fyne Salmon, Cucumber and Horseradish
by Jeremy Ford
Serves 10

350g Loch Fyne salmon fillets

300g smoked Loch Fyne salmon, diced

50g keta

1 egg white

350ml double cream

1 bunch chives

500g 00 flour

10 free range eggs

1 finger lime

1 cucumber

Skin from 1 whole salmon fillet

10ml olive oil

Salmon Mousse

Blend salmon fillets with egg white for 30 seconds, then pass through fine sieve.

Set over ice, then beat in cream gradually adding a little at a time. Season, then fold in diced smoked salmon, keta and chopped chives.

Cannelloni

Prepare 7 yolks and 3 whole eggs. Place flour and eggs into blender and pulse until well combined.

Remove and knead on flat surface for 2 minutes. Rest in fridge for 45 minutes.

Roll out dough to number 1 thickness on pasta machine. Cut sheets 10cm square and cook in boiling salted water for 30 seconds, then refresh in iced water.

When cooled, drain and trim to appropriate size. Dry and pipe in mousse, then roll in oiled cling film. Shape well then poach in water, just below simmering, until just set.

Compressed Cucumber

Peel cucumber, blend skin with a little water in spice blender. Strain liquid, which should be emerald green, into vacuum pack bag.

Cut 'sides' off cucumber lengthways, removing seeds and vacuum on full vac with cucumber water. Leave until cucumber turns translucent (up to 12 hours). Remove and cut into 5mm dice.

1 leek

50g Paris mushrooms

100ml white wine

500ml double cream

75g fresh horseradish, grated

2 star anise

10g coriander seeds

250ml fish stock

150g white fish trimmings

25g butter

1 lemon

2 bunches Easter radishes

30 fennel shoot leaves

15 breakfast radishes

300g Loch Fyne smoked salmon fillet

400ml good olive oil

100ml Muscatel vinegar

20g Dijon mustard

Crispy Salmon Skin

Ensure skin is free from any flesh and scales. Rub with a little olive oil, vacuum on full vac and cook in waterbath at 85°C for 3 hours. Refresh in iced water.

Remove from bag and gently roll out onto parchment paper. Allow to dry in dehydrator, very low oven or hot plate until crisp. Then deep fry at 180°C until it puffs up. Drain and salt lightly.

Horseradish Sauce

Finely slice leek and mushrooms. Wash well. Sweat in butter with star anise and coriander seeds. Then add fish trimmings and cook for 5 minutes. Add in wine and reduce to syrup, then add stock and reduce by half.

Add cream and grated horseradish then simmer for 5 minutes. Add juice of lemon and season. Pass through fine sieve.

Just before serving reheat without boiling and froth lightly with a hand blender.

To Finish

Carefully dice smoked salmon flesh into 5mm dice.

Finely slice Easter egg radish on mandolin and keep in iced water with fennel shoots.

Simmer breakfast radish for 30 seconds then refresh in iced water. Cut into small wedges.

For vinaigrette blend together olive oil, Muscatel vinegar and Dijon mustard. Season and set aside (use to dress radish).

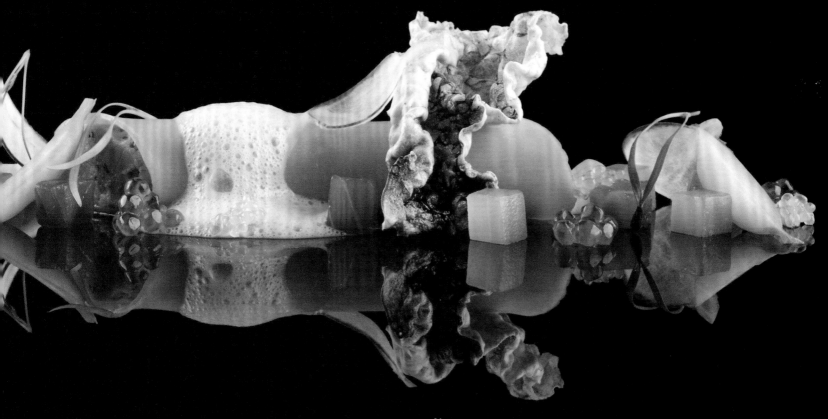

Cornish Mackerel, Heritage Beetroots and Orange by Jeremy Ford
Serves 10

10 small mackerel fillets
350g baby red beetroots
350g baby yellow beetroots
3 navel oranges
200g pomelo
400ml good olive oil
100ml Muscatel vinegar
20g Colman's English mustard
350ml orange juice
200g sugar
300g beetroot purée
30 pickled beetroot discs

3kg large red beetroots
4 cloves garlic
¼ bunch thyme
75ml balsamic vinegar
75ml olive oil
25g Maldon sea salt
50ml water
1ltr apple juice

200g sugar
15g star anise
15g pink peppercorns
15g coriander seeds
500ml white wine vinegar
500ml water
1kg Chioggia beetroot

Make house vinaigrette by blending together mustard, vinegar and oil. Season.

Cook beetroots in separate pans of salted water until cooked through. Chill, skin and either leave whole or cut in halves or quarters dependant on size. Dress in a little vinaigrette.

Wash oranges well, slice into 3mm thick slices and remove any pips. Bring to simmer in plain water and immediately refresh. Repeat twice more, then place into half orange juice, half sugar mixture and cook gently until orange peel is very soft.

Blend cooked orange adding in enough of cooking liquor and olive oil to emulsify, but leaving a soft purée consistency. Place into bottle for dressing or into piping bag.

Break apart pomelo flesh and remove cells for garnishing the dish.

To cook mackerel, score flesh and season with salt. Pan fry skin side down in non stick pan for 45 seconds until golden and skin is crisp. Turn over and pan fry for further 20 seconds to finish, making sure not to over cook the fish.

Beetroot Purée

Wash beetroots well and drain. Place beetroot in bowl with all other ingredients, except apple juice, and mix well. Make a parcel from foil to contain ingredients and seal securely.

Place in hot oven, 180°C, and bake for about 1 hour until beets are soft. Allow to cool.

Peel then slice beets into 1cm slices. Cover with apple juice and simmer until very soft.

Drain and blend in thermomix at 85°C until super smooth. Refrigerate until needed.

Pickled Beetroot Discs

Make pickling liquid by bringing all ingredients except for beetroot to simmer, then allow to cool.

Finely slice beetroot to 1mm thick slices, then cut out with round, size 3 cutter.

Place beetroot discs in sous-vide bag with pickling liquor and seal. Allow to pickle for 12 hours.

Squab Pigeon, Ras el Hanout, Butternut Squash, Hazelnut and Dates by Jeremy Ford
Serves 10

5 squab pigeons
20g ras el hanout spice
25g honey
100g noisette butter
50ml olive oil

250g shallots
5 pigeon carcasses
150ml Maderia
1 5cm piece of kombu
3 star anise
1ltr brown chicken stock

250g Japanese breadcrumbs
20g ras el hanout spice
5g salt

300g duck fat
10 pigeon legs
4 bay leaves
½ bunch thyme
100ml reduced pigeon sauce

Crown

Prepare pigeon by removing legs and leaving breasts on crown. Reserve all bones for sauce. Rub pigeon crown with a little olive oil and dust with about 2g ras el hanout spice. Trial and error will teach how much to add.

Seal on full vac and cook at 57°C for 45 minutes. Remove from bag and sear in hot pan with noisette butter. When golden add in spoon of honey, allow to bubble and reduce slightly. Coat breast well, rest for 5 minutes, then carve off the bone.

Brush the breasts with a little pigeon glaze.

Pigeon Sauce

Chop pigeon carcasses and roast in hot oven until well browned all over.

Caramelize finely sliced shallots with star anise until dark brown and well cooked. Add roast pigeon and Madeira and reduce to syrup. Add brown chicken stock and reduce by half. Remove from heat and drop in kombu. Cover and leave for 30 minutes, then strain and reduce to sauce consistency.

Spiced Japanese Breadcrumbs

Deep fry Japanese breadcrumbs in fryer of clean oil contained inside fine strainer. As soon as pale golden brown remove and drain well.

Add ras el hanout and salt whilst still hot. Mix well and allow to cool.

Legs

Remove thigh bone and neatly trim legs. Roll tightly in cling film to 'barrel' meat, then cook gently in duck fat with bay leaf and thyme at 90°C until cooked through.

Roll legs in pigeon glaze and then into fried, spiced Japanese breadcrumbs just before serving.

1 butternut squash	**Roasted Butternut Squash**
25g clarified butter	Cut discs of butternut 3mm thick and using a size 3, circular cutter cut out ten circles.
	Also cut 1cm dice. Poach both gently in salted water until cooked.
1 butternut squash	Pan fry in clarified butter until lightly golden brown and set aside.
45ml good olive oil	
15g Maldon sea salt	**Butternut Squash Purée**
150ml double cream	Halve squash and remove seeds. Rub a little olive oil and sea salt into flesh. Bake flesh side down on parchment paper until very soft.
250g hazelnuts	Scrape flesh from skin and purée in thermomix at 85°C for 5-6 minutes with double cream until super smooth.
1 punnet micro coriander	
10 large Grelot onions	**To Finish**
10 large dates	Roast hazelnuts in oven at 180°C until lightly browned, remove skins and allow to cool. Crack half the hazelnuts in half then shave the rest on a microplane or Japanese mandolin. Sprinkle over cooked pigeon breasts.
25ml good olive oil	

Roast hazelnuts in oven at 180°C until lightly browned, remove skins and allow to cool. Crack half the hazelnuts in half then shave the rest on a microplane or Japanese mandolin. Sprinkle over cooked pigeon breasts.

Place Grelot onions into vacuum pack bag with a little clarified butter and cook at 85°C for 20 minutes or until soft. Place into iced water until cool, then cut in half and sear in non stick pan to finish.

Skin and stone dates, cut into wedges and then roll into balls. Keep in olive oil.

Use micro coriander to garnish the dish.

Clark Crawley

Cooking has been in my blood from a very young age. I remember starting off making cakes with my mum, then moving onto more savoury flavours as I grew older.

I left school early to concentrate on my one true passion — food. At first I learned at home through books and the food network channel. I watched all the early cooking programmes over and over. Keith Floyd and the original Masterchef inspired me loads. Then as soon as I was old enough I completed a chef apprenticeship. That was it. I was on my way.

Since then I've been lucky enough to travel the world in cooking competitions and compete at the very highest level.

Cooking isn't rocket science. It's about having fun, experimenting and working at a level that satisfies your ambition.

Stone Bass with Charred Diver Scallop, Butternut Squash, Golden Raisins and Vanilla by Clark Crawley
Serves 4

4 x 150g stone bass
150g butter
50ml good olive oil
1 lemon
4 diver scallops

Trim stone bass to even portions. Check if any pin bones are left, if so remove. Score fish several times on skin side.

Cook bass by starting skin side down in oil in non stick frying pan. Add butter, turn fish and baste continuously. Then add a little squeeze of lemon.

Clean scallops by removing any connecting muscles and roe (so all that is left is pure white meat). Rinse and pat dry.

Chargrill scallops and finish in foaming butter.

500g butternut squash
10ml pumpkin seed oil
50g butter

Butternut Squash Purée

Peel butternut squash and remove seeds. Slice finely and sweat in pan with butter. Season. Stir, then cover with cartouche and cook down gently.

When soft, blend to super smooth purée whilst drizzling in pumpkin seed oil.

200g golden raisins
300g isomalt
600ml water
1 vanilla pod
25g citric acid

Raisins and Vanilla

Place scraped vanilla pod, isomalt, water and citric acid in pan and reduce to light syrup.

Add golden raisins and simmer for 5 minutes. Reserve to one side.

200g pumpkin seeds
200g isomalt
30g Maldon sea salt

Pumpkin Seed Croquant

In heavy bottomed pan, make a caramel with isomalt. When ready add pumpkin seeds and stir.

Pour onto greaseproof paper to harden. When completely cool, sprinkle with salt and chop thoroughly. Reserve in cool place.

200g button onions
800ml water
200g sugar
400ml white wine vinegar
2g peppercorns
3g bay leaves
4g thyme
2g mustard seeds
2g coriander seed
4g star anise
5g fresh red chilli

Pickled Onion Shells

Place all ingredients except baby onions into pan and reduce by half. Leave to infuse for 1 hour then strain.

Place onions into bag with pickling jus, vacuum and cook at 90°C for 20 minutes. Leave to cool in bag and refrigerate until needed, preferably overnight.

When ready to use cut onions in half lengthways and segment the layers. Reheat in a little pickle mix.

New Season's Grouse with Artichokes and Confit Savoy Cabbage by Clark Crawley
Serves 10

4 grouse
80g butter
5g thyme
1 bay leaf

Start by cleaning grouse. Remove head, feet and guts from the bird. Rinse the insides and pat dry. Keep the cleaned liver and heart to one side for the 'sausage roll'.

Remove legs and wings. Reserve legs for and wings for sauce.

Season two of the crowns well with salt and pepper. Brown in a pan and add butter, thyme and bay leaf. Baste and finish in the oven at 170°C for roughly 6 minutes.

Take breasts off the remaining crowns and set aside for the 'sausage roll'.

500g puff pastry
500g pork belly
4 grouse breasts
4 grouse livers and hearts
250g lardo
5g nutmeg, grated
200g shallots
10g thyme
300ml port
sherry vinegar
250g pancetta diced small
100g rusk
2 egg yolks
thyme
5g Maldon salt

Sausage Roll

Dice the shallots. Place in pan with the port and sherry vinegar and cook down until all the alcohol has dissolved.

Place the pork, grouse, livers, hearts, lardo, nutmeg, shallots, pancetta and rusk into a mincer. Season well.

Roll meat into 2.5cm width sausage and chill.

Lay out pastry and fill with the meat. Roll up, seal and glaze the top with egg yolk. Sprinkle with Maldon salt and picked thyme.

Bake in a hot oven until golden and cooked through.

8 grouse legs
5g marjoram
2 bulbs garlic
1 bay leaf
800g duck fat
100ml grouse jus
5ml truffle oil
10g tomato ketchup
100g Japanese breadcrumbs
2 egg yolks
50g flour
100ml good olive oil
25ml sherry vinegar
15g Dijon mustard

Bon Bon

Salt and marinate grouse legs with marjoram, garlic and bay.

Cook gently in fat until the meat falls from the bone.

When cooked pick the meat removing the skin and bones. Add the ketchup, truffle oil and jus. Roll into four evenly sized balls roughly 15g each. Chill.

Make house vinaigrette by blending together the mustard, vinegar and oil. Season.

Blend the panko to a finer crumb.

Pane the balls into flour, egg, then crumbs. Set aside and when ready to serve, fry until golden.

500g Jeruselum artichokes	**Caramelized Artichoke Purée**
100g butter	Peel and finely slice the artichoke.
100ml double cream	Bring butter to nut butter stage then add the
100g sugar	artichoke. Season and caramelize naturally in
50ml water	the pan.
50ml sherry vinegar	Separately caramelize sugar then add the sherry vinegar and water.

500g Jeruselum artichokes
100g butter
100ml double cream
100g sugar
50ml water
50ml sherry vinegar

Caramelized Artichoke Purée

Peel and finely slice the artichoke.

Bring butter to nut butter stage then add the artichoke. Season and caramelize naturally in the pan.

Separately caramelize sugar then add the sherry vinegar and water.

Add enough of caramel to the artichoke so it coats evenly. Cook gently for further 5 minutes.

Add double cream and simmer for 5 more minutes. Adjust seasoning and blend until smooth.

Set aside in a squeezy bottle until ready to use.

500g Jeruselum artichokes
350ml whole milk
150ml double cream
10g ultratex
0.8g gellem f
0.2g gellem lt 100

Artichoke Royale

Simmer the milk and cream and add salt to season. Thinly slice the artichoke, add to milk mix and bring back to the boil. Simmer for 5 minutes, then leave to steep in the liquid for 12 hours.

Strain milk mixture and bring back to a simmer. Thicken with ultratex until it becomes double cream consistency.

100g Jeruselum artichokes
200ml milk
1ltr oil for frying

Place in thermomix with the rest of the gellem powders. Blend at 100 degrees for two minutes. Pour into flexi moulds to set.

When ready to serve, re-warm the royales in their moulds, covered in clingfilm in a steamer.

Artichoke Crisps

Wash and dry artichokes well.

Thinly slice artichokes by length and place in milk for 10 minutes.

Deep fry artichokes at 160°C until golden. Season and set aside.

1 Savoy cabbage
50g bicarbonate of soda
50g banana shallots
100g duck fat
4g thyme
25g butter

Confit Savoy Cabbage

Using only dark leaves of cabbage, remove stalks and shiffanade as thinly as possible.

Boil water and bicarbonate together, season and cook cabbage as quickly as possible, slightly over cooking (the cabbage should break up if pinched). Refresh in iced water. Drain and dry.

500g salsify
250ml red wine
250ml port
100g damson jam
50ml raspberry vinegar
100g butter

Gently confit shallots and picked thyme for 10 minutes until soft. Add cabbage, season and cook down. Finish with butter.

50g butter
8 grouse wings
2 grouse carcasses
100g shallots
4g thyme
1 bulb garlic
50g carrots
50g mushroom trimmings
50ml sherry vinegar
100ml Madeira
400ml veal stock
400ml chicken stock
2g tarragon
2g chervil
50g plum tomatoes

50g grouse skin
1g salt
1ltr oil for frying

Port Glazed Salsify

Peel salsify and sand down with a clean scourer pad. Cut into 5cm batons.

Submerse salsify in wine, port, vinegar and damson jam. Reduce gently until the salsify is cooked and jus is to a syrup consistency.

Finish with butter, and allow to melt and emulsify into sauce.

Game Jus

Caramelize thinly sliced shallots and carrots in butter with a pinch of salt very slowly for 30 minutes.

Then add mushroom trimmings, thyme and garlic. Caramelize for further 10 minutes.

Meanwhile, chop and roast the carcasses, then add to the shallot mix.

Deglaze with sherry vinegar, add the Madeira reduce, then add stocks and simmer gently skimming all the time for about 1 hour.

Strain through fine muslin, then put back on stove to reduce gently with the fresh herbs, tomato and roasted grouse wings. Skim, skim, skim!

When reduced to desired taste and consistency, pass through a superbag.

Puffed Skin Powder

Clean skin and pin out flat into vacuum bags. Seal on full vac and cook sous-vide at 85°C for 2 hours.

Then pin skin out onto a non stick tray and dehydrate until dry and fully crisp.

Deep fry in clean oil at 190°C.

Season and chop roughly to form a puffed powder.

Salt Pollock with Parsley and Lemon Crust, Manchego Purée, Confit Garlic and Tempura Squid with Espelette Pepper by Clark Crawley
Serves 4

5 x 130g pollock
100g Maldon salt
25ml good olive oil

Start by removing skin of fish, rub liberally with all the salt and set aside in fridge for 2 hours. Rinse thoroughly, then place in vacuum pack bag with a little olive oil.

Crust:
100g parsley
1 lemon, zest and juice
50g Parmesan
50g butter
50g breadcrumbs
3g cayenne

For crust, place all ingredients into food processor and blend until smooth and bright green. Roll out between two greaseproof papers until 5 mm thick. Chill until firm, then cut out to size that will cover pollock.

When ready for service, cook pollock at 52°C for 15 minutes in waterbath. Remove from bag, lay onto baking sheet and top with crust. Place under grill for 1 minute then serve.

Manchego Purée

400g Manchego
500ml whole milk
10g gelespessa

Grate Manchego and simmer very gently with milk for 1 hour.

Blend with gelespessa to stabilize the mix.

Place in squeezy bottle and place aside, keeping warm until serving.

Confit Garlic

100g red waxy potatoes
200g crème fraiche
40g ultratex
12 bulbs garlic
200ml olive oil
3g thyme

Bake potato in oven at 180°C for 45 minutes until soft. When ready, pass through fine drum sieve and set aside.

Blanch garlic twice, then confit gently for 1 hour with oil and thyme. Set aside 8 bulbs for pan roasting later on. They will be used as garnish. Purée remaining garlic and mix with potato purée.

Warm crème fraiche and thicken with ultratex. Mix together with potato mixture until super smooth. Season and place into piping bag.

Tempura Squid

200g baby squid tentacles
100g cornflour
100g plain flour
20g baking powder
75ml white wine vinegar
400ml sparkling water
10g espelette pepper
5g salt

Prepare squid and leave to one side.

Make batter by mixing remaining ingredients, except espelette pepper, together.

When ready to serve, dip squid into batter and fry as quickly as possible at a high heat.

Season with salt and espelette pepper.

350g frozen peas
100ml extra virgin olive oil
100g butter
½ bulb garlic
100ml water
5g basil
1 lemon

1 pollock skin
50ml olive oil
200ml good olive oil
1g coriander seeds
4g thyme
1g peppercorns
1 bay leaf
1 bulb garlic
1g star anise
200g Heritage tomatoes
20g basil
20g shallots
50ml Chardonnay vinegar
50g Kalamata olives

40g breakfast radish, shaved
15g pea shoots
½ punnet edible flowers
2g espelette pepper

Crushed Peas

Cook peas in plenty of boiling, salted water.
Drain well and crush peas with a fork or masher and set aside.

Gently soften garlic by sweating in hot oil, add water and simmer for 10 minutes. Add peas and season, then stir in butter until melted and emulsified. Finally add in basil and lemon juice when ready to serve.

Fish Skin Crisps

Place pollock skin in vacuum pack bag and cook at 85°C for 2 hours. Chill.

Pin out skin onto tray, season, then place heavy tray on top and bake at 160°C until crisp (roughly 10 minutes).

Break into shards and set aside.

Tomato and Olive Vierge

Infuse coriander, thyme, peppercorns, bay leaf, garlic and star anise in oil and leave overnight. Pass through fine strainer.

Dice shallots and cook down with vinegar.

De-seed and peel tomatoes. Dice to 1cm squares. Pick basil leaves off stalks and finely slice. Neatly dice olives.

Mix everything together and dress with infused oil.

To Garnish

To serve, reheat pollock under the grill. Spread a little Manchego purée on plate with a small step palette knife.

Place fish on top surrounded by confit garlic, finely sliced radish, crushed peas and pea shoots.

Finally add crispy skin and sprinkle a little espelette pepper over plate.

John Killington

Cooking has always been my passion, and I count myself fortunate to spend my working life doing something I love so much. It's a privilege to work with fantastic produce that inspires me to continue creating new and exciting dishes. There's no greater satisfaction than when a customer says that the food I've cooked for them is the best they've ever had.

I've been lucky enough to work with some fantastic chefs over the years, and travelled to some amazing countries. And knowing how these experiences have influenced my cooking has in turn given me the desire to pass on my knowledge to the next generation of chefs.

So I love to teach. Today, I'm involved with running workshops in a primary school. It's a real joy to see children showing an interest in food, and learning how great it can be.

Herb Crusted Fillet of Halibut, Gnocchi, Artichoke and Summer Beans by John Killington
Serves 10

10 x 120g halibut fillets
400g small white bloomer
120g parsley
120g basil
2 lemons
175g butter

Remove crusts from bread and discard. Blend bread in food processor until becomes breadcrumbs. Add basil and parsley and blend again until green. Add softened butter, lemon zest and seasoning. Blend until a paste forms.

Place between two sheets of greaseproof, roll flat to 2-3mm and place in fridge until set. Cut to shape of halibut fillet, refrigerate until needed.

To cook, season halibut, place in hot frying pan and seal for 2 minutes. Place a sheet of herb crust on top, remove paper then put in oven at 180°C for 4 minutes. Remove, add a squeeze of lemon and serve.

650g Maris Piper potatoes
160g 00 flour
2 egg yolks
30g Parmesan, finely grated
Salt and pepper

Gnocchi

Place potatoes on salted baking tray and bake at 180°C until cooked.

Once cooked, scoop flesh out and put through drum sieve. Mix in flour, egg yolks, Parmesan and seasoning and mix to a dough.

Roll gnocchi into long sausage on floured surface and cut into 2.5cm lengths.

Blanch in salted boiling water for 2 minutes. Set aside for service.

1.5ltr fish stock
750ml white wine
4 banana shallots
½ bulb fennel
1 leek
4 garlic cloves
1 lemon
¼ bunch lemon thyme
60ml good olive oil
500ml double cream
2 tbls Sosa pro espuma

Fish Velouté

Sweat all vegetables, garlic and thyme in olive oil, without colour.

Add white wine and reduce to syrup. Then add fish stock and reduce by half. Add double cream and reduce by half. Pass through fine strainer.

Before service, reheat, add pro espuma and lemon juice. Froth with a hand blender.

600g broad beans, shelled
2 banana shallots
150ml double cream
25g butter
2g salt
2g pepper

Broad Bean Purée

Sauté sliced shallots in a little butter until translucent. Add broad beans keeping 100g back for garnish. Season, cover with just enough simmering water to cover and cook for 5 minutes.

Drain beans. Warm cream. Blend beans in thermomix adding cream until mixture is a smooth paste. Pass through fine sieve and season.

150g runner beans
150g bobby beans
25g butter
2 punnets baby San Marzano tomatoes
1 clove garlic
½ bunch basil
Salt and pepper
90ml olive oil

Beans and Tomatoes

Prepare and blanch beans. Reheat in a little butter and season before serving.

Blanch tomatoes and remove skins. Chop garlic and place on baking tray with basil. Place tomatoes on top, drizzle with olive oil and season. Leave in oven at 70-80°C for 1 hour.

To Finish

To finish the dish, prepare samphire by removing any woody stalk and blanch. Prepare oyster leaves by removing any black leaves and wash.

½ punnet sea herbs, oyster leaves and samphire

Quail, Pancetta, Baby Carrots and Orange Salad with Fig Tart by John Killington
Serves 10

10 quails

10 sprigs lemon thyme

2 cloves garlic, finely sliced

250g duck fat

200g Pancetta, sliced

(½tsp meat glue) transglutomate

1 chicken breast, skinned and boned

1 egg white

225ml double cream

2g salt

30g chives

500g carrots

10g butter

2 banana shallots

2 cloves garlic

1 lemon, juiced

200ml double cream

5 figs

100ml stock syrup

2.5g agar agar

1 lemon

500g puff pastry

5 figs

100g apricot jam

1 egg

Quail Preparation

Remove wishbone and legs from body. Take one leg, French trim drumstick and remove thigh bone.

Oil and lightly salt inside of thigh. Roll in cling film to form sausage shape and tie both ends. Confit in duck fat at 70°C for 1 hour. Remove and cool in fridge.

Debone other leg. Place between two sheets of cling film and flatten with meat press until double the size. Pipe chicken mousse mix down middle of leg flesh side, dusted with meat glue. Roll in cling film, tie both ends and place in sous-vide bag and waterbath for 1 hour at 65°C. Remove.

Remove breast from crown. Lay out Pancetta slices and wrap breasts individually. Place in sous-vide bag with a little oil, lemon thyme and sliced garlic.

Cook in waterbath at 50°C for 20 minutes. Remove.

Remove legs and breast from packing and season. Sauté legs in butter for 5 minutes. Add breasts to pan. Cook all for further 3 minutes and serve.

Chicken Mousse

Blitz chicken breast in blender for 30 seconds. Add egg white and salt. Blitz for further minute.

Chill mixture for 15 minutes. Push mixture through drum sieve then slowly add cream.

Season and add chopped chives.

Place in piping bag ready for quail leg.

Carrot Purée

Peel carrots and chop finely. Slice shallots and garlic. Put them in warm pan with butter and season. Cook for 5 minutes. Add a little water, cover and cook until tender.

Purée carrots in blender until smooth. Add warm cream and lemon juice. Pass through fine sieve, check seasoning and keep warm.

1ltr chicken stock

4 quail carcasses

2 medium oranges

250ml Maderia

50ml good olive oil

2 bunches baby carrots,
yellow and red

3 medium oranges

30g lemon thyme

4 cloves garlic

5g Maldon salt

15g caster sugar

125g pea shoots

Fig Gel

Chop up figs. Juice and zest lemon.

Add stock syrup and cook until a purée. Pass through fine sieve and blend in agar agar. Cook for 2 minutes.

Place in container and set in fridge. Remove jelly from fridge and blend until a gel with hand blender. It may need a little water to help.

Place into piping bag.

Tart

Cut pastry into 10 rectangular shapes 2cm x 6cm, stud with fork and egg wash. Place a little fig gel on pastries. Slice figs and place on top.

Bake between two baking trays for 20 minutes at 175°C or until golden brown. Glaze with a little melted apricot jam.

Orange Dressing

Roast off quail bones, add to pan and add Maderia. Reduce by three quarters.

Add chicken stock and reduce until jus consistency. Pass through fine sieve.

Reduce juice of two oranges in pan by half. Add jus and whisk in olive oil. Check seasoning.

Carrot and Orange Salad

Segment oranges and leave to one side. Peel carrots and cook in pan of water with lemon thyme, garlic, salt and sugar for 5 minutes.

Remove and slice carrots. Mix with orange segments to make salad.

Finish dish with garnish of pea shoots.

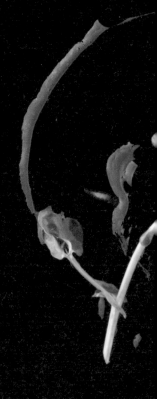

Seared New Forest Venison Carpaccio, Croquette, Wild Mushrooms, Celeriac and Red Wine by John Killington
Serves 10

1.5kg venison loin
10g juniper berries
1 orange, zested
20g Maldon salt
30g thyme
20g fennel seeds
30ml good olive oil

1kg venison haunch
1ltr red wine
20g juniper berries
30g thyme
10g star anise
5g black peppercorns
20g smoked paprika
1 stick celery
500g carrots
3 banana shallots
5 cloves garlic
30g tomato paste
30g parsley
1.5ltr veal stock
120ml good olive oil
Salt and pepper
3 eggs
100g plain flour
150g Japanese breadcrumbs
200ml milk

Venison Loin Carpaccio

Trim loin of venison to remove any silver skin and fat.

In a pestle and mortar, grind spices, herbs, orange zest and salt together. Oil venison and rub on ground spice mix. Leave for 1 hour.

Sear venison in hot pan with a little oil. Remove from heat and cool. Wrap loin tightly in cling film and place in freezer overnight ready for slicing.

Remove from freezer, slice thinly and place on plate.

Croquettes

Marinade venison leg in red wine overnight with chopped vegetables, garlic, herbs (excluding parsley) and spices.

Remove venison leg and vegetables from marinade and place venison in hot pan. Season with salt and smoked paprika. Seal all sides then remove and place in a deep baking tray.

In same pan, cook vegetables and add tomato paste. Cook for 2 minutes, add red wine marinade and reduce by half. Add veal stock and pour over venison and vegetables. Cover and braise in oven for 2-3 hours at 120°C or until tender.

Remove leg and set aside. Reduce cooking liquor by three quarters and pass through a muslin ready for sauce and croquettes.

To make croquettes, break down venison, add chopped parsley and a little of the sauce to moisten venison. Place venison onto cling film. Roll tightly into a ballotine. Place in fridge.

Remove and cut into 1cm discs. Coat in seasoned flour, egg, milk and breadcrumbs. Deep fry at 175°C until golden brown. Season.

1ltr red wine	**Red Wine Syrup**
500ml water	Add red wine, water, sugar, garlic, star anise, bay leaves and thyme to pan and reduce to syrup.
250g caster sugar	
10g star anise	Add an equal amount of venison sauce to syrup to make dressing.
10 bay leaves	
3 sprigs of thyme	
2 cloves garlic	

Wild Mushrooms

300g wild mushrooms	Sauté prepared mushrooms in olive oil in hot frying pan. Cook for 2 minutes. Add diced shallots and garlic. Cook for further 2 minutes. Season.
1kg banana shallots	
2 cloves garlic	Add vinegar and chopped chives. Remove from pan ready for service.
40ml Cabernet Sauvignon vinegar	
30g chives	Blanch plum tomatoes, skin and remove seeds then cut flesh into neat dice. Add to mushrooms.
2 plum tomatoes	
2g salt	
2g pepper	
20ml good olive oil	

Celeriac Purée

	Cut three quarters of celeriac into 1cm dice, keeping trimmings. Slice remaining quarter of celeriac thinly on mandolin.
2 celeriac	With leftover trimmings, finely chop for purée. To make purée, add sliced shallots and garlic to warm pan with knob of butter. Cook for 2 minutes. Add celeriac trimmings,
50g baby watercress leaves	
10g rosemary	season and cook for further 2 minutes. Cover with white chicken stock and milk and cook until tender.
400g banana shallots	
4 cloves garlic, crushed	Heat double cream in separate pan. Remove celeriac from pan and place in blender with cream until smooth consistency. Then pass through fine sieve. Check seasoning and adjust if necessary.
50g butter	
150ml double cream	To cook diced celeriac, warm butter in pan. Add celeriac and rosemary, then season. Place in oven at 180°C and cook for 10 minutes or until soft.
500ml white chicken stock	
500ml milk	Deep fry the celeriac slices at 165°C until golden and season with salt. Finish dish with baby watercress.

Gary Rhodes OBE

My desire to cook and spend my life in the kitchen began at a very young age, tugging at my mother's apron. In those days we didn't have flavours flown in from around the world 365 days a year. Instead, simple cooking concepts changed with the seasons. Often the year would begin with slow braising, lead through to light salads and bites, and then give way to classic roasts.

But my true inspiration came from reading George Orwell's Down and out in Paris and London. There were no glossy celebrity chefs. The only celebrity was the dish itself. As I read I could feel the tension, the pressure, the ups and downs, the continual buzz of the hot sweaty room. I could almost hear the oven doors clashing. I loved it and wanted to become part of it - a professional chef.

That feeling has lived on throughout my working life. I've realised I'm absorbing a continual culinary education, always wanting to learn a little bit more. That's what keeps on injecting drive and passion. You realise that true love and inspiration are not only born from the heart, but also continue to motivate as it beats.

During many foodie travelling days, one thought I heard has always stayed with me: "The road to success is always under construction."

Crème Caramel by Gary Rhodes OBE
Serves 6

1 vanilla pod
500ml full cream milk
225g caster sugar
2 eggs
80ml egg yolks

Lightly grease six ramekin moulds.

Scrape seeds from vanilla pod, add to milk and bring to boil. Remove from heat and infuse for 20 minutes.

Put half the sugar in a pan and add enough water to level with sugar. Simmer to golden colour.

Pour enough caramel into each ramekin to cover base and leave to set.

Preheat oven to 150ºC.

Beat remaining sugar, eggs and yolks. Re-boil the milk and pour over eggs, stirring well. Strain into ramekins.

Place the dishes in roasting tin and two thirds fill tin with water. Cook for 40-45 minutes until set.

Leave to cool in fridge for 6-8 hours before turning out.

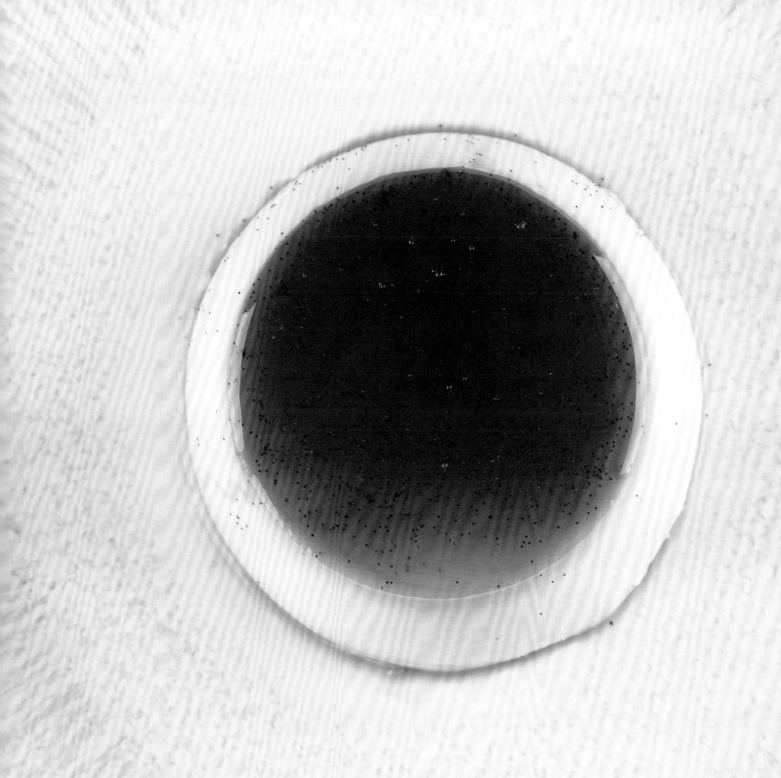

Seared Halibut with Blood Orange and Courgette by Gary Rhodes OBE
Serves 4

700g halibut fillets
30g flour
30ml olive oil
30g butter
1 lemon
300g courgettes
3 blood oranges, segmented
70g red onion, finely sliced
40g basil
2g salt
2g pepper

6 oranges, juiced
10g caster sugar
50ml olive oil
2g salt
2g pepper

Peel courgettes lengthways into long strips.

Pat dry fish on kitchen paper and dust with flour. Season with salt and pepper.

Heat oil in hot pan and fry fillets for 5-8 minutes, turning in pan. Add butter and when sizzling add squeezed lemon juice and baste fish.

Mix courgettes with orange segments, sliced onion and basil leaves. Add some dressing and fold together.

Divide salad between 4 plates and place fish fillets on top.

Dressing

Boil orange juice with sugar down to 100ml. Cool, then whisk in oil and season.

Mandarin Tart by Gary Rhodes OBE
Serves 6

600ml mandarin juice
2 mandarins
6 eggs
100g caster sugar
150ml double cream
30g icing sugar
400g sweet pastry

125g butter
250g flour
2g salt
75g icing sugar
40ml egg yolks
25ml water

Line a 30cm tart ring with pastry, lay over some baking parchment and fill with baking beans or rice. Refrigerate for 20 minutes.

Blind bake for 20 minutes on 175°C. Remove baking parchment and re-bake for further 5 minutes at lower temperature of 150°C.

Zest mandarins and boil mandarin juice and zest rapidly, reducing to 175ml. Cool.

Beat eggs and sugar together, add mandarin juice and cream. Pour into pastry case.

Bake for 50 minutes until just set. Leave to cool completely before removing from tart ring.

Dust with icing sugar and caramelize with blow torch.

Sweet Pastry

Cut butter into small pieces and leave to soften at room temperature.

Sift flour and salt onto work surface. Make well in centre and add butter and sugar. Work into fine crumbs.

Add egg yolks and slowly add water forming into smooth dough. Do not overwork.

Wrap in cling film and rest in fridge for 2 hours before using.

Chris Pulfer

There was a time when I wanted to become a policeman. At 5ft 6 that was never going to happen. Otherwise I knew from a very young age that I wanted to be in the food scene.

I've always looked to achieve perfection in whatever I've done, whether it's a simple weekend dinner or a complex dish in the professional kitchen. There's just been something inside from the early days. A passion. A desire to succeed.

I've been fortunate to have worked in some amazing kitchens alongside so many great chefs. Beginning to understand their individual stories has really inspired me. Being with people who are truly passionate about what they do, in places where food is paramount, are the foundations that inspire me to what I do each and every day. It's a mix of all the perfect ingredients.

Banham Chicken Breast, Gnocchi, Baby Leeks and Confit Chicken by Chris Pulfer
Serves 10

10 Banham chicken breasts
2 bunches baby leeks
200ml jus
1 bunch Grelot onions
50g butter

Trim chicken breasts of bone. Season and pan fry until golden and cooked through.

Blanch baby leeks in salted water. Refresh in iced water until needed.

Blanch onions until soft and reserve until needed.

Heat baby leeks and baby onions in a little butter and season.

Heat jus and pour over chicken.

Confit Chicken Wings

30 chicken wings
1ltr chicken stock
100g leeks
100g carrots
1 stick celery
100g white onions
40g thyme
2g salt
2g pepper

Trim and clean chicken wings.

Trim, wash and peel vegetables. Cut into rough 2cm pieces.

Sauté chicken wings in hot pan to golden colour. Add vegetables and thyme and colour. Pour on chicken stock.

Gently simmer for 2-3 hours until bones can easily be removed.

Press chicken between two trays and place heavy weight on top. Press overnight.

Trim wings into neat rectangles and fry until golden. Season.

Gnocchi

1kg potatoes
200g 00 flour
100g Parmesan, finely grated
8 eggs
20g egg yolks
2g salt
2g pepper

Cook potatoes in hot oven until soft. Whilst still warm, scoop out and pass through a fine sieve.

Gently mix eggs and flour together, slowly incorporating potato and cheese.

Roll into thin rolls on floured board and cut into 1cm pieces. Leave to rest in fridge for 1 hour before using.

Drop gnocchi into boiling salted water and cook until they rise to surface. Refresh in iced water and drain.

Pan fry in foaming butter for service and correct seasoning.

Garlic Purée

500g garlic
50ml olive oil
150ml double cream
50ml milk
40g unsalted butter
2g salt
2g pepper

Coat garlic cloves in oil and butter and wrap tightly in foil.

Bake at 140°C until tender, about 1 hour. Remove skin and purée until smooth.

Bring double cream and milk to boil and add to purée until velvet smooth consistency is achieved. Season with salt and pepper.

Garlic Crisps

20 cloves garlic
250ml milk

Peel and slice garlic cloves as thinly as possible.

Bring milk to simmer and drop garlic slices in for 30 seconds. Drain well and dry out in dehydrator or very low oven until crispy.

North Atlantic Cod, Ibérico Croquette and Piperade by Chris Pulfer
Serves 10

Pea Purée

1kg peas
200g shallots, finely sliced
20g thyme
20g garlic, crushed
30g unsalted butter
300ml double cream
2g salt
2g pepper

Blanch peas in plenty of seasoned, boiling water until soft and bright green. Drain peas and refresh immediately into iced water. Drain and reserve.

Sweat shallots and thyme for 2 minutes in butter. Add garlic and cook for further 2 minutes.

Add cream to pan and bring to boil.

Add peas to blender with a little of cooking liquor and cream and blend until smooth. Season with salt.

Pass through strainer and reserve until needed.

Croquette

300g plain flour
50g unsalted butter
400ml milk
50g Ibérico ham
25g flat leaf parsley
2g nutmeg, finely grated
200g Japanese breadcrumbs
2 eggs
2g salt
2g pepper

Melt butter, add 175g of flour and make roux. Cook out.

Heat milk with nutmeg and add slowly to roux. Whisk well to smooth, thick consistency.

Cut ham into a fine 1mm dice and finely chop parsley. Fold into mix. Correct seasoning and chill to set in greaseproof lined tray.

Cut the set croquette mix into 1cm x 6cm pieces.

Dip into flour, egg and then breadcrumbs. Repeat process to cover croquettes well.

Deep fry until golden.

Piquillo Pepper Sauce

100ml chicken stock
10ml red wine vinegar
3 Piquillo peppers
100g cherry tomatoes on vine
20g basil
20ml double cream
30ml olive oil
2g salt
2g pepper

Reduce stock by half. Add vinegar.

Blend with peppers, tomatoes, basil leaves and oil. Pass through fine strainer to smooth consistency.

Correct seasoning.

Add cream and whisk to aerate.

Cod Fillet

1kg cod fillets
30g Maldon salt
34g caster sugar
1 lime
10g thyme
50ml olive oil

Trim cod fillets and remove all bones.

Zest the lime and mix with sugar, salt and thyme leaves. Rub salt mix over cod and leave in fridge for 3 hours.

Wash fillets and pat dry. Place in sous-vide bag with oil and hard seal.

Cook in preheated waterbath at 55°C for 10 minutes.

Remove from bag and pan fry skin side down until crisp.

Red Peppers

400g red peppers
20g thyme
200g banana shallots
2g salt
2g pepper
20ml olive oil

Roast pepper in hot oven until blackened. Remove skin and cut flesh into julienne.

Finely chop shallots and sweat in oil without colour for 2 minutes.

Add pepper strips and thyme leaves. Cook slowly on low heat for 20 minutes stirring from time to time.

Correct seasoning and keep warm until needed.

Rillette of Loch Fyne Salmon, Pickled Cucumber and Sourdough by Chris Pulfer
Serves 10

400g salmon fillets
80ml olive oil
100g crème fraiche
50g sour cream
20g dill
20g chives
1 lemon, juiced

Salmon Rillette

Cut salmon fillet into 4 x 100g pieces and place in individual sous-vide bags.

Add 20ml of olive oil to each bag and hard vacuum.

Preheat waterbath to 50°C and cook salmon for 15 minutes. Place into iced water.

Remove salmon from bag and gently flake.

Finely chop dill and chives. Mix salmon with remaining ingredients.

300g wholemeal flour
50g oatmeal
200ml natural yoghurt
20g unsalted butter
2g bicarbonate of soda
2g Maldon salt
30g caster sugar
200ml whole milk

Sourdough

Grease tins with a little butter.

Combine flour, oatmeal and butter. Rub to form a texture like breadcrumbs.

Add bicarbonate of soda, salt and sugar and mix.

Make a well and add milk and yoghurt. Do not over mix.

Place in tin and sprinkle with a little oatmeal.

Cover with foil and bake for 25 minutes at 200°C. Remove foil and bake for further 15 minutes at 200°C.

1 cucumber
50g caster sugar
100ml Muscatel vinegar
2g Maldon salt

Pickled Cucumber

Peel then slice cucumber lengthways into thin strips using peeler or mandolin.

Bring caster sugar, Muscatel vinegar and salt to simmer. Cool completely.

Add cucumber slices to vinegar solution. Marinade for 20 minutes and then strain.

Nick Whatmough

To begin with, cooking fascinated me from a scientific point of view. It was only later that it developed into a real passion. I love the concept of taking something from nature and creating it into a clever meal that makes a truly memorable experience.

I think provenance and sustainability are incredibly important. I always try to use any produce I can from the West Country to support my heritage.

I love to create dishes that are vibrant, full of flavour and visually stunning. My inspiration comes from nature, so I'm always looking for new ways to represent it in my presentation.

Mushrooms on Toast by Nick Whatmough
Serves 4

4 x 2.5cm slices sourdough
200g girolles
100g trompettes
100g ceps
100g chestnut mushrooms
100g pied bleu
20ml Madeira
120g banana shallots
25ml good olive oil
1 clove garlic
5g thyme
5g tarragon
5g lemon zest
4 quails eggs
50g unsalted butter

200g girolles
100g trompettes
100g ceps
100g chestnut mushrooms
100g pied bleu
125ml Madeira
200ml water
1 clove garlic
¼ bunch thyme

4 slices of sourdough bread
4 portions cooked mushrooms
6 quail's eggs, soft boiled
25g Parmesan, shaved
12 sprigs chervil
2 large ceps, cleaned and cut in half
40ml mushroom reduction
25g butter

Toast sourdough slices on both sides.

Prepare mushrooms and check for large clumps of dirt. Wash in a volume of water three times the quantity of mushrooms and repeat three times until all grit and dirt has been removed. Use salad spinner to remove excess water from mushrooms. Spin until no more water appears in bottom of spinner. Leave mushrooms on tea towel at room temperature until completely dry.

Finely chop shallots and garlic and sauté off in olive oil until translucent. Remove from heat, add lemon zest, picked thyme and tarragon. Set aside to cool.

Cook quail eggs in gently boiling water for 2 minutes 30 seconds. Chill in plenty of cold water and peel, then cut in half and season.

Pan fry ceps in oil until golden. Deglaze with Madeira, put on plate and allow to rest. Pan fry remaining mushrooms in oil. Once they start to colour, add ceps, shallot mixture and 30g of butter. When butter starts foaming, reduce heat, baste mushrooms and season. Once cooked drain on paper towel.

Add another 20g of butter to pan and pan fry sourdough very quickly to absorb butter and remaining mushroom juice.

Mushroom Reduction
Sweat mushrooms in small pan with roughly chopped garlic and thyme until nicely golden. Deglaze with Madeira, add water and bring to simmer.

Simmer for 10 minutes and skim off any impurities. Cover with foil and cook for 8 hours at 85°C (low oven).

Afterwards pass through muslin and reduce to thick sauce consistency.

Plating Guide
Divide cooked mushrooms between the four pieces of grilled and fried sourdough bread.

Garnish with soft boiled quails eggs and shaved Parmesan.

Place assembled 'mushroom on sourdough' onto flat round plates.

Pan fry halved ceps in foaming butter, season and add to the plate.

Finally top with reduction and small pieces of picked chervil.

Braised Guinea Fowl Leg Pie by Nick Whatmough
Serves 10

5 whole guinea fowl

1ltr chicken stock

75ml Madeira

25ml brandy

100ml Bellevue bordeaux (red wine)

2 carrots

2 shallots

30g thyme

1 bay leaf

25ml tomato ketchup

5ml soy sauce

10ml Worcestershire sauce

5ml Tabasco sauce

3ml truffle oil

300g plain flour

125g butter, room temperature

5g sugar

4g salt

1 egg

60ml whole milk

1 egg

10ml water

8 baby purple beetroots

35ml ruby port

35ml Cabernet Sauvignon vinegar

70ml olive oil

2g salt

5 Chioggia beetroots

5 golden beetroots

35ml white port

35ml Muscatel vinegar

70ml olive oil

2g salt

10 guinea fowl breasts

20g salt

6g pepper

12 cloves garlic

12 sprigs thyme

150g butter

30 baby turnips

30 Heritage baby carrots

250g kale

Pastry and Guinea Fowl

To make the pastry, pulse flour, butter, sugar and salt in food processor to combine. Next whisk egg and add to flour mix. Pulse again to combine. If pastry feels too dry add milk as required in two tablespoon additions.

Prepare guinea fowl into breast and leg portions. Chop the carcasses into 2.5cm pieces. Reserve the breasts for main dish. Roughly chop carrots and shallots.

Caramelize legs off in heavy based saucepan and set aside. Add carcasses to this pan along with roughly chopped vegetables. Continue to cook until caramelized. Deglaze with Madeira, brandy and red wine. Place legs in top of pan, add chopped bay leaf and sprig of thyme. Cover with chicken stock ensuring legs are completely submerged by stock. Bring to simmer and skim. Cover with foil and place in oven at 165-170°C for 2½ hours, then check to see if more cooking is required.

If not, allow legs to cool. Reduce cooking liquor to sauce consistency and pick down braised meat from just the legs avoiding tendons and gristle.

Combine ketchup, soy sauce, Worcestershire sauce, Tabasco, truffle oil and half the braising sauce (reserve the other half for the dish). Adjust seasoning with salt if necessary.

Line 6cm diameter, non stick, mini pie dishes with pastry (use 7cm cutter diameter). Blind bake until fully cooked. Cut 7cm diameter lids with remaining pastry. Cool before adding braised mix and use egg yolk to help stick lid to pie.

Cut a cross in pastry lids to let out excess moisture and bake for 15-20 minutes at 170°C until fully cooked. When removed from oven, glaze with a light egg wash and return to oven for 2 minutes to set egg wash. Cool on wire rack.

Beetroots

Combine port, Cabernet Sauvignon vinegar, olive oil and salt. Trim tops of baby beetroots and place in sous-vide bag. Vacuum pack, removing all air and place in waterbath on 90°C for 1 hour until cooked. Then plunge into iced water to cool.

Remove beets from bag and place in blender and blend until very smooth. Add some of the cooking liquor and extra oil, if required, until it's a very smooth purée consistency.

Combine white port, Muscatel vinegar, olive oil and salt and place the baby golden and Chioggia beets into separate sous-vide bags. Vacuum pack, removing all air and place in a waterbath on 90°C for 1 hour until cooked. Cut to appropriate shapes.

To finish

Blanch baby turnips for 2-4 minutes until just tender. Chill, and peel with sharp knife.

Blanch Heritage baby carrots for 2-3 minutes. Chill and then use a clean scourer to remove skin.

Blanch kale for 1 minute and refresh.

Cut all vegetables to required shape and size.

Season guinea fowl breasts with salt and pepper and pan fry until golden. Add garlic, thyme and butter, then cook in oven skin side down for 5 minutes at 160°C. Turn breasts and cook for another 2-4 minutes until cooked. Rest for 10 minutes.

Crab Tian by Nick Whatmough
Serves 4

1.6kg cock crab
50g crème fraiche
2 red chillies
20g chives
1 clove garlic
100g banana shallots
1 lemon
A few drops to taste Tabasco sauce
5ml Worcestershire sauce
2g Cornish sea salt

Cook crab for 7 minutes in gently boiling water. Remove and rest for 10 minutes, then chill quickly with ice.

Once cool, break down crab separating white and brown meat. Reserve brown meat for beignets.

De-seed and finely chop red chillies. Finely chop shallots, garlic and chives. Zest the lemon.

Stir fry shallots and garlic with no colour. Remove from heat and add chilli, lemon zest and chives. Leave to cool.

Check white crab meat for shell and cartilage, then combine all other ingredients including Tabasco and Worcestershire sauce.

Finally season to taste.

Brown Crab Beignet

20ml milk
22g unsalted butter
45ml water
1g salt
1g sugar
37g flour
1½ eggs
Pinch of cayenne
4 drops Worcestershire sauce
50g brown crab meat
10g Parmesan, finely grated
15g Japanese breadcrumbs

Combine milk, butter, water, salt and sugar over very low heat. Add flour to form dough and knead in mixer until cool.

Once cool, add eggs a bit at a time while mixing on high speed with paddle. Beat for 5 minutes. Lower to medium speed.

Pass brown crab meat through fine drum sieve and add to mixture. Then add cayenne and Worcestershire sauce to taste.

The mixture should be a thick paste. Rest in fridge for 1 hour.

After an hour incorporate Parmesan and Japanese breadcrumbs. Oil two tablespoons and quenelle. Deep fry at 180°C.

Red Gazpacho Purée

3 red peppers
200g red cherry vine tomatoes
300ml orange juice
1g salt
5ml Muscatel vinegar

Chop and de-seed half the peppers. Remove skins from the other half using a blow torch. Remove blackened skin ensuring none is left.

Finely chop peppers and tomatoes. Mix with orange juice and place in heavy bottomed pan allowing the liquid to cover all ingredients.

Gently simmer until orange juice has reduced by two thirds and ingredients are soft.

Drain and blend in a blender until very smooth. Add some cooking liquor if too thick, then season with salt and Muscatel vinegar to taste.

Tiger Tomato Bread

242g strong flour
37g rye flour
7g fresh yeast
156ml water
7g salt
7g honey
7ml olive oil
45g semi dried tomatoes, puréed
4 whole crab shells

Combine flours, rub in yeast and add water.

Add salt, honey, olive oil and puréed semi dried tomatoes. Knead for 5-9 minutes until elastic and coming away clean from bowl. If it's not, add a tablespoon of strong flour and continue mixing until you get a clean bowl. Form into round ball, wrap in cling film and leave to double in warm place.

Once doubled in volume, knock back and form into log, dividing into 55g portions.

Place into crab shells and spray with water. Cover with cling film.

Combine all ingredients for tiger crust and roll to 1mm between two sheets of greaseproof. Chill.

Cut to desired shape and place on tomato dough in shell at beginning of proving process. This allows crust to crack as bread doubles in volume again.

Tiger crust:
50g rice flour
50g Japanese breadcrumbs
5g fresh yeast
12g honey
6ml oil
90ml water

Once doubled in size, cook at 200°C with oven on 25% moisture. After 13 minutes turn tray and reduce temperature to 180°C for another 10 minutes.

To check if the bread is ready, tap it. It should sound hollow and be golden in colour.

Michel Roux Jnr

Cooking food and wine is not
just a passion it's a way of
life. No other craft can bring
such joy and happiness to the
consumer and the creator.

Lobster by Michel Roux Jnr
Serves 4

4 lobsters
2 shallots
1 carrot
1 stick celery
1 clove garlic
1 piment d'espelette (dry chili)
30g tomato purée
60ml brandy
250ml white wine
120ml mirin paste
4 sticks lemon grass
60g butter
100ml coconut cream
50g fresh coconut flesh
60ml double cream
60ml olive oil
750ml fish stock
Salt and pepper

Boil lobster in boiling salted water for 4 minutes. Take out and leave to cool. Crack open and cut flesh into bite size medallions.

Break up bones and shells and place in saucepan with a little olive oil. Add chopped shallots, carrot, celery, garlic, chilli and lemon grass. Sweat this for 6-7 minutes, then deglaze with brandy followed by wine and mirin.

When almost dry add stock and tomato purée. Simmer for 20 minutes, then pass through fine sieve.

Boil this to reduce by half then finish with coconut cream and double cream.

Gently reheat lobster in a little melted butter, check seasoning and arrange on plate on a bed of lemon purée, seaweed tagliatelles and slithers of fresh coconut.

Lemon Purée

3 unwaxed lemons
75g sugar
75ml water
3g salt

Use lemons that are as fresh as possible.

Simmer sugar and water for 2 minutes to make stock syrup.

Blanch lemons ten times changing water each time, then leave to cool a little. Cut open and remove any pips. Place into blender and purée until smooth, adding stock syrup to taste and a little salt.

The purée should be sharp and slightly bitter sweet.

Seaweed Tagliatelle

60g salted kombu, rinsed and dried
500g 00 flour
5 egg yolks
3 eggs

Blitz seaweed and flour to breakdown and then add eggs.

Knead and rest for 20 minutes. Roll out through a pasta machine, cutting with the tagliatelle attachment.

Chocolate Marquise by Michel Roux Jnr
Serves 10

5 egg whites

255g caster sugar

75g ground almonds

12g milk powder

124g flaked hazelnuts

500g extra bitter Valrhona chocolate

500ml double cream

20ml dark rum

20ml crème de menthe

40g crystallized ginger, chopped finely

12 After Eight mints

125g caster sugar

25ml water

125ml double cream

Biscuit

Whisk egg whites until frothy then add 180g sugar. Continue to whisk until firm, then fold in the ground almonds, remaining sugar and milk powder.

Spread onto lightly buttered and floured greaseproof paper to thickness of 5mm. Sprinkle with flaked hazelnuts and cook at 180°C for 20 minutes or until just set.

Leave to cool then cut into strips 8cm wide.

Ganache

Melt chocolate in bain-marie without it reaching more than 35°C. Whip cream up to light ribbon, then pour half of the melted chocolate onto cream and mix well with whisk. Gently add remaining chocolate.

Divide the mixture into three. Flavour two portions; one with rum, the other with crème de menthe.

Layer marquise starting with strip of biscuit followed by rum ganache speckled with ginger, then biscuit followed by mint flavoured ganache and chocolate mints. Use plain ganache to encase marquise with 1cm layer.

Place in fridge to set for at least an hour. Cut into 2cm slices, decorate with white and dark chocolate curls and caramel sauce.

Caramel Sauce

Dissolve sugar in water and gently bring to simmer. Cook until a deep caramel colour is reached.

Pour in double cream and allow to bubble. Reduce heat and cook until all caramel has dissolved. Strain and allow to cool.

Pig's Head on Toast by Michel Roux Jnr
Serves 10

1 pig's head, split including
tongue
1 onion
1 stick celery
1 carrot
2 bay leaves
35g spring thyme
4 pig's cheeks
4 cloves garlic
Salt and pepper

15g clear honey
15g grain mustard
240ml hazelnut oil
120ml sherry vinegar
1 baguette bread
1 clove garlic
60g toasted hazelnuts, crushed
Salt and pepper
Mixed baby leaves
1 green apple, cut into
matchsticks
4 shallots, roasted in skins

Place cleaned pig's head and cheeks in pan with aromatic garnish. Cover with cold salted water and bring to very gentle simmer for 2 hours or until tender.

Leave to cool in liquid. When cool enough to handle, carefully remove bones and lay one half of head skin down on tray lined with cling film. Pick meat off skin from both halves along with cheeks and tongue. Pull to shred.

Add sliced ears then season well with salt and pepper and moisten a little with some reduced cooking liquor.

Smear this on top of skin, then carefully place other half on top. Cover with cling film and weigh down in fridge to set.

Salad
Blitz shallots until smooth to make a purée.

Make dressing with honey, vinegar, mustard and oil. Season lightly with salt and pepper.

Cut a thin slice of baguette and toast, then rub this with clove of garlic.

Slice a piece of pig's head 1cm thick and place onto baguette.

Re-heat in oven or grill.

Dress salad leaves, apple, toasted hazelnuts with dressing.

Place warmed pig's head toast onto spoon of shallot purée on the plate.

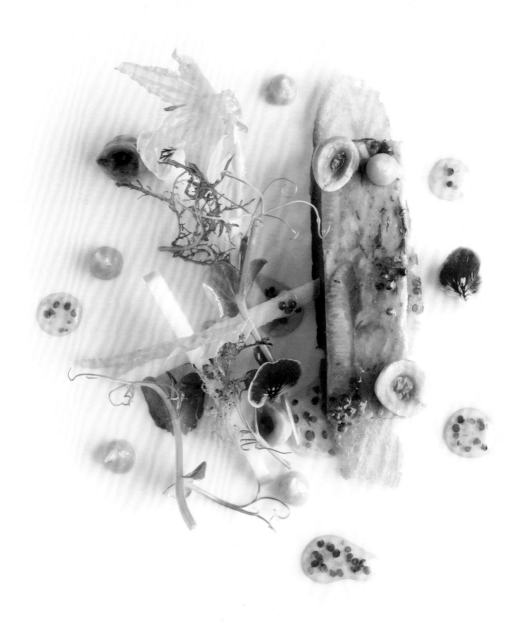

Paul Dunstane

You know, I've never really had a sense of direction or a clear path to follow. As one job has naturally come to an end, there's always been another interesting and exciting opportunity that's strengthened me and taken me up to the next level.

One thing's for sure though. Nearly thirty years on I still love what I do - whether it's working in the kitchen with my brigade, experimenting with food at home, creating new dishes, learning new techniques or simply talking to new suppliers.

Service time still has a profound buzz for me. Creating something that's gone in an instant for someone else's pleasure is an amazing, even a humbling feeling … and my passion and drive for doing that really well have never faded.

Slow Roasted Gressingham Duck Breast, Gizzards, Spiced Cherries, Beets and Turnip by Paul Dunstane
Serves 10

10 whole ducks
100g beetroot purée
150ml duck sauce
50g confit gizzards
1 large turnip
20g pistachios
10 duck pastillas
200g spiced cherries
Half head fresh endive
100ml rapeseed oil
15g thyme
1 bay leaf
30g garlic
15g rosemary
10g cinnamon sticks

10 duck legs
400g Maldon sea salt
45g thyme
20g juniper berries
15g garlic
1.5ltr duck fat
5g black peppercorns
1 pack paté a brick
2 eggs
1 bay leaf

Prepare ducks by removing legs for confit. Take out wishbones and remove breasts. Chill in fridge for 20 minutes. Then trim off any excess fat and score skin close together with sharp knife. Chop carcass, remove all fat and roast until golden brown ready to refresh finished duck sauce.

To plate the dish, begin by slow roasting duck breasts in non stick pan with small amount of rapeseed oil, thyme, garlic, bay leaf, rosemary and cinnamon stick. Slowly render on skin side only until all fat is removed and skin is crisp and golden. Turn once onto flesh side and cook until pink. Rest duck breasts while you prepare rest of garnish.

Slice the turnip 3mm thick and cut out circles with a 2cm round cutter, dress with house vinaigrette.

Warm beetroot purée, duck sauce and spiced cherries.

Thinly slice duck gizzards on Japanese mandolin and set aside.

Fry duck pastilla and rest on tray with duck breast.

Dress plate with warm beetroot.

Trim duck breast to make one thick slice and lay onto beetroot purée. Garnish plate with cherries, endive, pastilla and pistachios.

Warm duck sauce and add roasted duck carcass to refresh, pass off, check seasoning and finish with knob of butter.

Dress plate with finished sauce.

Crisp Duck Pastilla

Make confit salt by placing salt, thyme, juniper, garlic, bay leaf and black pepper in a food processor and coarsely blend.

Evenly rub both sides of duck legs with confit salt and leave covered in fridge for 2 hours. Then wash under cold running water and pat dry.

Melt duck fat, place duck legs in suitable container to confit in oven and cover with the warm duck fat. Cover container with foil, place in oven at 140°C and cook until meat leaves the bone easily. This could be up to 2 hours.

Drain legs from oil and while still warm flake meat from bone and place in clean bowl. Bind with a small amount of warm duck fat. Check seasoning and roll into a cylinder 1.5cm thick and 12cm long using cling film. Chill in fridge until completely set.

Wrap the duck confit in the paté a brick using egg wash to seal edges. Keep for service.

Beetroot Purée

500g red beetroots
100ml beetroot juice
60ml Cabinet Sauvignon vinegar
6g Cornish rock salt
60ml olive oil

Roast beetroots in olive oil and salt, wrapped in foil at 180°C until soft.

Peel beetroots while still warm, chop roughly and transfer to a blender with remaining ingredients.

Blend until you have a smooth purée.

Duck Sauce

2kg fresh duck bones, chopped to 2.5cm
200g banana shallots, finely sliced
200g button mushrooms, finely sliced
10 cloves garlic, split in half
10g fresh thyme
1 fresh bay leaf
150g unsalted butter
350ml white wine
400ml dry Madeira
1.2ltr white chicken stock
1.2ltr brown chicken stock
100ml spiced cherry juice

Roast duck bones in tray at 180°C until golden brown. Remove from oven and drain.

In large, heavy bottomed pan heat butter until nut brown. Add mushrooms and shallots and caramelize, adding garlic for last 10 minutes. Drain in colander.

Deglaze the tray and pan with white wine then reduce by half. Add Madeira and bring to the boil.

Transfer all ingredients to suitable pot with the bay leaf, and slowly bring to simmer, skimming any impurities and fat.

Simmer for 2 hours repeating the skimming.

Pass through a colander, then tap through a fine strainer lined with muslin. Leave to chill.

Remove any excess fat and reduce to sauce consistency.

Finish sauce for service with some cherry juice and a knob of butter.

Confit Gizzards

100g duck gizzards
20g salt
20g sugar
100ml duck fat

Mix salt and sugar and season the prepared gizzards.

Leave to marinate for 6 hours.

Wash and pat dry.

Place gizzards in small vacuum pack bag and add duck fat. Seal bag and cook in waterbath at 55°C for 72 hours.

Take out of waterbath and chill until needed for service.

Hand Dived Scallops, Cauliflower, Spices and Curried Raisins
by Paul Dunstane
Serves 10

15 hand dived scallops
10ml olive oil
5g salt
50ml rapeseed oil
75g butter
1 lemon
15g sea salt
10 portions cauliflower purée
10 portions cauliflower and almond cous cous
10 portions curried raisins

Open scallops, reserving the white skirts, wash well, drain and pat dry.

Caramelize scallops in rapeseed oil and finish with foaming butter and freshly squeezed lemon juice. Season with sea salt.

Place on to draining cloth to drain any excess butter, and keep warm.

Dress plate with warm cauliflower purée. Add scallops to plate.

Finish dressing plate with cauliflower and almond cous cous, curried raisins and crisp scallop skirt.

10 scallop skirts, rinsed well under running water for 30 minutes

Crisp Scallop Skirt

Place scallop skirts in vacuum pack bag with a little olive oil. Cook in waterbath set to 85°C for 3 hours, then cool in bag.

Remove from bag and dehydrate in dehydrator or alternatively in low oven at 80°C for

1-2 hours until crisp.

Deep fry until lightly golden and salt lightly.

1 cauliflower
13g salt
150ml double cream
100ml milk

Cauliflower Purée

Prepare the cauliflower by removing stalk and cutting into small florets. Place cauliflower and salt in large sous-vide bag. Steam for 15 minutes.

Drain in strainer and transfer to blender.

Add remaining ingredients and blend to smooth purée.

1 cauliflower
100g almonds
5g sea salt
1 lemon
25ml extra virgin olive oil

Cauliflower and Almond Cous Cous

Trim cauliflower florets to remove stalk and blend in food processor to size of cous cous.

Roast almonds in hot oven, 180°C for 6 minutes, or until light golden brown. Allow to cool then blend to same size as cauliflower.

Blanch cauliflower in boiling salted water and refresh. Drain when cooled.

Mix cauliflower with almonds and season to taste with fresh lemon juice, sea salt and olive oil.

1 Granny Smith apple, sliced finely
50g banana shallots, sliced finely
10g Madras curry powder
2g star anise
5g black peppercorns
75ml white port
5g lime leaves
5g salt
50g golden raisins
15ml canola oil

Curried Raisins

In medium, straight sided sauté pan, heat canola oil over medium heat. Add apple and shallots and sweat until translucent without caramelizing (about 10 minutes).

Add curry powder, star anise and peppercorns. Toast with apples and shallots for about 1 minute.

Deglaze pan with port and reduce until pan is almost dry. Add a cup of water and lime leaves. Bring to boil. Remove from heat, steep for 10 minutes and season with salt.

Place golden raisins in heat proof container, strain hot liquid over raisins and cool to room temperature.

Keep raisins in liquid until needed.

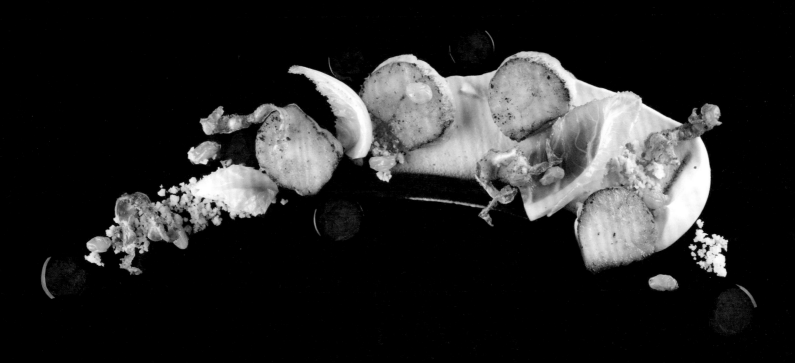

Sea Bream with Artichokes, Salsify and Cep Mushrooms
by Paul Dunstane
Serves 10

10 salsify ribbons
500g Jerusalem artichoke purée
125ml red wine reduction
500g salsify and hazelnut purée
10 sea bream fillets
200g ceps
300g cavolo nero
20 sprigs Bronze fennel
20 leaves Buckler sorrel
100g Jerusalem artichokes

1.5ltr red wine
165g black grapes
75g caster sugar

200g salsify
120ml good olive oil
10g caster sugar
5g salt
1 lemon

250g Jerusalem artichokes
3.5g salt
75ml double cream
50ml milk

200g salsify
15ml lemon juice
80ml double cream
2g salt
35g Sosa hazelnut paste

Red Wine Reduction

Blitz grapes with 500ml red wine. Add to remaining 1000ml red wine. Sous-vide for 24 hours.

Pass through muslin and reduce with sugar until temperature reaches 116ºC.

Transfer to squeezy bottles.

Salsify Ribbons

Place all ingredients in sous-vide bag and cook in waterbath for 1 hour at 85°C.

Once cooked, place bag in an ice bath to cool.

To serve, remove from bag and peel with speed peeler.

Jerusalem Artichoke Purée

Place artichokes and salt in large sous-vide bag. Steam for 40-60 minutes, or until very tender.

Drain in strainer. Transfer to blender.

Add remaining ingredients and blend to a smooth purée.

Salsify and Hazelnut Purée

Place salsify and cream in large sous-vide bag with salt. Cook in steamer for 1 hour.

Once fully cooked, drain and transfer to blender. Add hazelnut paste.

Blend, adding back enough liquid to make a smooth purée.

Finish with lemon juice.

To serve

Arrange sea bream, purées, crushed artichokes, cavolo nero, red wine reduction, salsify ribbons, ceps, artichoke crisps and micro herbs on the plate.

Michael Lipscombe

When I was seven, I spent a weekend away in Margate with my family. The rest of them were all enjoying cod and chips at a seafront fish and chip shop. Not me. I was tucking into shark.

Food has always intrigued me. The earth is rich with amazing produce. Pumpkins in winter. Asparagus in spring. Berries in summer. Hearty game in autumn. In every season, there's so much inspiration all around us.

I love to create, to cook, to taste, to indulge, and to be part of something special. The smell of freshly baked bread mid-morning is the one of the greatest in the world. The cracking of the toasted crust, the light aroma that scents the room … good food shared around a table with family and friends.

Just like my family, food and cooking mean the world to me. They're why I get up every morning with a smile on my face. I'm lucky to be part of something magical. I have a passion, not just a job.

The beauty of working with Restaurant Associates and their dedicated team of Chefs is that one day I might be cooking for the most prestigious names in industry and the next for a classroom of hungry children, both require and get the same level of attention to detail.

Lemon Sole by Michael Lipscombe
Serves 10

5 lemon soles

4 heads broccoli

1 Romanesco

200g cobnuts

2 large Désirée potatoes

150g samphire

50g sea purslane

1 lemon

250g butter

5g salt

Gut, fillet and skin fish. Trim down to size.

Pan fry in hot pan. Baste with butter, squeeze with lemon and drain.

Finely slice broccoli, using no stalk at all. Blanch in salted water for 2-3 minutes. Drain and blend in a blender. Pass through a strainer and chill over ice bath to retain colour.

Prepare the Romanesco to small florets. Blanch in salted water and refresh in iced water.

Take cobnuts out of shells and pan fry in foaming butter and salt.

Pick sea herbs, removing any woody stems. Blanch and refresh.

Peel potatoes and cut into fine strands on a vegetable lathe. Heat up clarified butter. Season and dress potato strands in clarified butter. Wrap piece of greaseproof paper around a copper pipe about 1 cm in diameter. Carefully start to wrap potato around pipe to form a spring-like shape. Deep fry at 190°C until potato is golden brown. Remove from oil, cool for few seconds and with oven cloth pull out copper bar. Snap potatoes into required size springs.

Red Mullet by Michael Lipscombe
Serves 10

5 x 800g red mullet
2g Maldon salt
200g olive oil

Mullet

Scale, gut and fillet mullet, removing pin bones. Next skin the fish.

Portion to 150g (5oz), neatly trimmed fillets. Place in vacuum pack bag with some olive oil and season. Cook in waterbath at 50°C for 13 minutes.

200g Scottish girolles
125ml Muscatel vinegar
40g Demerara sugar
20g clear honey
125ml water

Pickled Girolles

Trim girolles.

Boil all other ingredients with water. Pour over girolles and chill. Leave to steep for minimum of 2 hours

10 mullet skins

Mullet Skin

Ensure skins are free from any flesh and scales.

Vacuum on full vac and cook in waterbath at 85°C for 3 hours. Refresh in iced water. Allow to dry and then deepfry at 180°C until golden.

1 Crown Prince pumpkin
100g butter
100ml double cream

Pumpkin Purée

Peel pumpkin and slice thinly. Sweat down in butter, season and add a touch of water. Cook until soft. Add cream, re-boil and blend in thermomix.

3 plum vine tomatoes
15ml Muscatel vinegar
Pinch of salt
6g sugar

Tomato Petals

Blanch, refresh, peel and de-seed tomatoes. Cut into random shapes, dress in Muscatel vinegar and season with salt and sugar. Dry under lights.

250g runner beans

Runner Beans

Peel side off beans and blanch in salted water. Refresh in iced water and reserve.

2 oxtails, sectioned
1kg carrots
1kg onions
6 cloves garlic
¼ bunch thyme
1ltr red wine
2ltr veal stock

Oxtail Cannelloni

Peel and cut all vegetables and mix with oxtail along with all other ingredients (apart from veal stock). Leave this to marinade for 24 hours.

Pour marinaded ingredients into colander to drain, reserving liquid. Fry oxtail in hot frying pan until well browned, then repeat with vegetables.

Reduce wine by three quarters, add veal stock and bring to simmer. Place all in vacuum pack bag and cook at 85°C for 24 hours. Drain off liquor and reduce.

580g 00 flour
12 free range egg yolks

Pick meat from oxtail and fold in reduced liquor. Roll in cling film and chill.

Pasta

Blend eggs and mix into flour to form smooth dough. Knead, then rest.

Roll into pasta sheets, drop into boiling salted water with a little oil for 30 seconds. Refresh in iced water until cooled. Drain.

Wrap the pasta sheets around the oxtail meat and then into cling film. Poach gently to reheat.

Lobster and Cauliflower by Michael Lipscombe
Serves 10

10 x native lobster (each
weighing 500g)

200g Morecambe Bay shrimps

30g nasturtium leaves

1 lemon

500g butter

2g Maldon salt

200g clarified butter

2 cauliflowers

500ml milk

500ml cream

3 eggs

10 lobster nuggets

10ml truffle oil

500g Désirée potatoes

4 Italian eggs

100g potato flour

2g Maldon salt

Lobster

Blanch lobsters in salted water for 1 minute then place straight into iced water to release from shell.

Cut shell through length of 'belly'. Place into individual vacuum pack bags with 20g clarified butter in each bag and cook at 59.5°C for 15 minutes. Keep warm.

Reserve claw nuggets for cauliflower mousse.

Pick nasturtium leaves and use for garnish when plating up.

Wash shrimps. Add butter to hot pan and when it starts to foam add whole, unpeeled shrimps and cook for 3-4 minutes, keeping the butter foamy. Squeeze on lemon and add salt. Drain.

Cauliflower Mousse

Cut cauliflower as thinly as possible (reserve a quarter of cauliflower for mini florets). Cover with cream and milk, and season. Cook until soft and blend in thermomix to silky smooth then pass through fine strainer.

Measure out 250ml of purée and chill. Keep remaining purée for plating the dish.

Blanch florets.

Take the 250ml of cauliflower purée and blend in two whole eggs, one yolk and truffle oil. Fold in lobster nuggets. Check seasoning and transfer to piping bag with small nozzle. Pipe onto sheet of cling film then wrap up to form a tube.

Roll and tie ensuring there are no air bubbles. Place a J-cloth in bottom of pan, add rolls and cover with cold water. Place another J-cloth on top to ensure the rolls are submerged.

Bring slowly up to simmer then pull pan off the heat and leave mousses in the water for 20 minutes.

Place mousse rolls into another bowl of cold water, still in cling film. Reserve until needed. When serving, place in pan of hot water for 5 minutes to reheat, then remove from cling film.

2k lobster bones
3 celery sticks
600g shallots
1 bulb fennel
600g carrots
300g leeks (white parts only)
6 plum tomatoes
2 bay leaves
1 orange, zest in thin strips
10g parsley
10g tarragon
40g tomato purée
3 star anise
30g fennel seeds
30g pink peppercorns
20g coriander seeds
50ml brandy
1g saffron
21tr fish stock
11tr brown chicken stock
10g Sosa elastic

21tr lobster stock
70ml egg whites
200g fish trimmings
50g carrots
50g celery
50g leeks
50g onions

Gnocchi

Wash potatoes and bake in jackets at 160°C for 45 minutes.

Pass through fine sieve.

Mix all ingredients apart from mash to smooth paste. Add mash, put into piping bags and chill for 1 hour.

Lay out sheets of cling film and pipe on long rolls of the mix. Tie up, then chill.

Steam for 20 minutes at 80°C.

Lobster Jelly

Chop and lightly oil lobster bones. Roast at 170°C until golden.

Peel all vegetables apart from tomatoes and caramelize. Add bones and tomato purée.

Deglaze with brandy and reduce. Cover with the stocks.

Toast all dry spices in hot pan and add to lobster stock with orange zest, tarragon, bay leaf and parsley.

Simmer for 2 hours, skimming regularly. Pass through fine muslin cloth.

To set the jelly, measure 500ml stock and add 10g of Sosa elastic. Blend with hand blender.

Put in pan and reheat to 85°C, skimming any impurities away. Ladle onto tray to 3mm deep and allow to set. Once set cut to required size.

Clarification for Stock

Pulse fish trimmings in food processor then blend the carrots, celery, leeks and onions to a paste. Mix together and add egg whites. Add lobster stock and bring to simmer very quickly, whisking every few minutes so clarification mix does not stick to bottom of pan.

When crust starts to settle on top, reduce heat right down. Once crust has formed make small hole and simmer for 15 minutes.

Gently ladle out cleared stock through muslin cloth.

Neil Rankin

All I've ever wanted to be is a pastry chef. That's what I am now, so it's easy to say that I love what I do. My job has taken me all around the world - so inspiration has always been there on tap from the variety of cultures that I've worked in.

Whether it's a dessert, a petit fours or a simple sour dough, it all comes down in the end to one thing … and that's pleasing someone.

White Chocolate Mousse, Passion Fruit and Coconut by Neil Rankin
Serves 10

70ml water

45ml glucose syrup

2½ leaves gelatine, soaked

280g white chocolate

200ml UHT whipping cream, semi whipped

200ml water, boiling

800ml passion fruit purée

60g Sosa pro crema 100

125g caster sugar

Acetate sheet

200g Valrhona Manjari chocolate 64%, tempered

Sticky tape

250ml coconut purée

12g Sosa vege gel

135g passion fruit purée

3 eggs

135g caster sugar

4g agar agar

175g butter, diced

300g jumbo oats, sieved to remove powder

300g honey

100g desiccated coconut

100g flaked almonds

Sosa passion fruit crispy

Chocolate Mousse

In a pan, place water and glucose on medium heat. Meanwhile melt chocolate.

Once water is boiling add drained gelatine. Stir and pass through fine strainer onto melted chocolate, stirring only in middle to create an elastic core and smooth emulsion.

Making sure chocolate mix is at temperature of 37-50°C, start to add cream one third at a time.

Once all cream is incorporated, chill for minimum of 2 hours.

Passion Fruit Semi Sorbet

Dissolve sugar in water, then add purée and pro crema. Blend with hand blender and set aside in fridge for minimum of 4 hours to mature.

Pour into pacojet beaker and freeze for minimum of 12 hours before processing.

Chocolate Tube

Pour teaspoon of chocolate onto 10cm x 10cm piece of acetate. Spread with palette knife leaving a 1cm strip clear down one side.

Lift acetate and roll over the chocolate covered edge to the clean edge and slide it to make a seal with the other end of chocolate sheet.

This should form a cannelloni shaped tube.

Fasten with a little sticky tape. Allow to set, repeat 10 times to make 10 tubes.

Fill centre of tube with chocolate mousse and passion fruit curd.

Coconut Fluid Gel

Place coconut purée in pan with vege gel. Stir continuously until boiling. Transfer to container and chill until cold.

Blend until smooth in thermomix and pass through fine strainer.

Passion Fruit Curd

Place purée, eggs, sugar and agar agar in pan. Cook on medium heat until mixture reaches 84°C.

Transfer to thermomix and blend on speed 7, adding butter slowly.

Once all the butter is incorporated, transfer to fridge until required.

Granola

Mix all ingredients (apart from passion fruit crispy) and bake on tray at 160°C, checking every 3-4 minutes and stirring.

Once golden remove from oven and allow to return to room temperature. Then add passion fruit crispy. Reserve in airtight container.

Strawberry Cheesecake by Neil Rankin
Serves 10

300g good quality cream cheese
100g caster sugar
200ml UHT whipping cream
1 vanilla pod

Cream Cheese

Place cream cheese in mixer bowl with sugar and seeds from vanilla pod. Beat until smooth with the paddle.

Add cream and keep beating until a light pipeable mix is formed.

1.36kg strawberries, hulled
396g icing sugar
1tbls Kirsch

Strawberry Sorbet

Mix all ingredients together and leave for 20 minutes.

Blitz mixture in blender until smooth and pass through fine strainer.

Churn in ice cream machine.

400g strawberry purée
100g caster sugar
1 lemon, juiced
30g Sosa vege gel

Strawberry Jelly Sheet

Place all ingredients in pan on medium heat and whisk slowly until boiling.

Pour mix onto metal tray whilst angled at 45°. This will create a thin film of jelly. Once set cut into desired shape.

400g strawberries, hulled
20g caster sugar
20ml water

Compressed Strawberries

Place all ingredients into vacuum pack bag. Seal on maximum pressure and leave for at least 2 hours.

400g butter
200g milk powder
30g icing sugar

Brown Butter Crumb

In pan, start to melt butter then add milk powder stirring continuously as it can catch very easily.

Keep cooking until it is golden in colour. Pass through strainer and place solids on tray to cool.

Once solids have cooled but are still a little warm, place them into thermomix with icing sugar and blend until a fine crumb is obtained.

Reserve in airtight container.

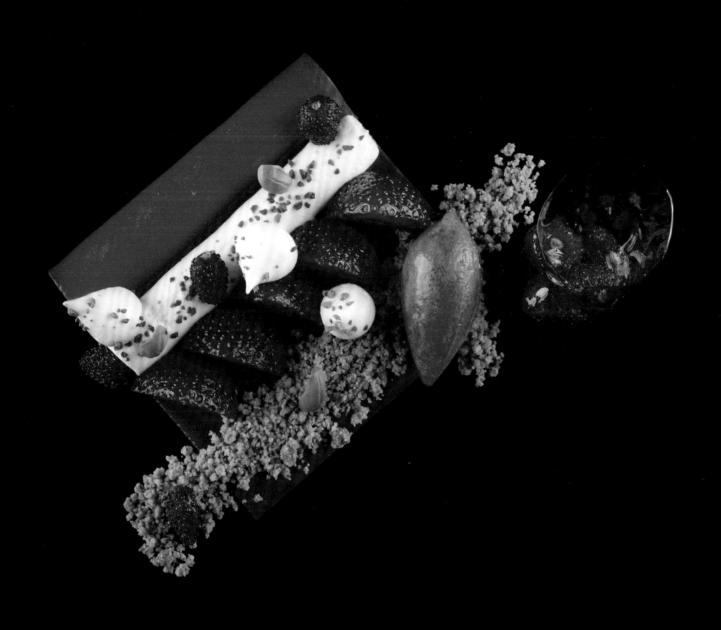

Granny Smith Apple, Tapioca, Ginger and Tarragon
by Neil Rankin
Serves 10

5 Granny Smith apples
50g atomised glucose
300g caster sugar
700ml water, boiling
60ml fresh lemon juice
10g tarragon
30g Sosa pro-crema 100

1 Bramley apple
1 fresh vanilla pod
200g caster sugar
10g vitamin C powder

500ml fresh apple juice
30g Sosa vege gel

90g tapioca
1 vanilla pod
1ltr milk
100g sugar

150g unsalted butter, chilled
and diced
150g soft flour
150g Demerara sugar
150g ground almonds
50g Valrhona Eclats D'or
12g ground ginger
1 lemon, zested

2 Granny Smith apples
20ml apple juice

Apple Sorbet

Quarter the unpeeled apples and freeze overnight.

Take boiling water (re-measure once boiled, add more to make up to 700ml) and dissolve rest of ingredients in water.

In thermomix, blend frozen apple, tarragon and syrup together bit by bit.

Pass apple mix through fine strainer pushing with the back of ladle, then pass a second time without a ladle.

Set mix aside in fridge for minimum of 4 hours to mature.

Churn in ice cream machine.

Bramley Purée

Peel and chop apple quickly. DO NOT put in acidulated water.

Split vanilla pod and scrape the seeds out.

In a plastic bowl, place apple, sugar, vitamin C and vanilla pod/seeds. Microwave until completely cooked (approximately 8-10 minutes).

Remove vanilla pod, blend in thermomix and pass through a fine strainer.

Chill purée with cling film touching the surface to stop skin forming.

Apple Jelly

Place juice and vege gel in pan and bring to boil.

Pour hot liquid immediately onto flat tray placed at 45° angle, aiming to cover as much of tray as possible with a thin sheet of jelly.

Place in fridge until making tapioca roll.

Tapioca

Place tapioca, split vanilla pod and half the milk in heavy based saucepan. Cook slowly. As tapioca starts to thicken add a little more milk (you may not need all the milk).

Once cooked, add sugar and chill straight away.

Take chilled tapioca and pipe 8cm strip onto apple jelly. Cut jelly and roll it over like a cannelloni. Reserve to one side in fridge.

Ginger Streusel

Place all ingredients in mixer bowl. Mix with beater until a light crumb is formed.

Bake at 150°C for 8-10 minutes until light golden.

Compressed Apple

Peel and dice apple. Vacuum pack dice and juice on full vacuum setting for minimum of 2 hours.

Fromage Frais Mousse with Citrus and Yoghurt Meringue by Neil Rankin
Serves 10

150g egg whites
280g caster sugar
Sprinkle of Sosa crispy yoghurt
Sprinkle of Sosa acidic yoghurt powder

Meringue

Place egg whites and all sugar in bowl. Whisk over bain-marie until mix is approximately 64°C.

Then transfer egg/sugar mix to mixer and whisk on speed 6 until cold.

Take meringue and pipe onto silicone paper, then spread with palette knife until you have desired size.

Sprinkle with crispy yoghurt and yoghurt powder. Dry out at 80°C for about 2-3 hours in oven.

400g fromage frais
100g UHT whipping cream
2½ gelatine leaves, soaked in cold water
125g egg whites
250g sugar
100ml water

Mousse

Boil sugar and water to 118°C. Meanwhile, whisk egg whites in mixer at speed 6.

Once whites have doubled in size reduce speed and add the 118°C sugar slowly. Then increase speed back to 6. Whisk until cold.

Boil cream and then add drained gelatine. Once dissolved, add one third of fromage frais to gelatine mix. Mix well.

Add rest of fromage frais and meringue alternately. Then reserve in fridge until needed.

1 pink grapefruit
1 ruby grapefruit
10 physalis
1 large orange
1 blood orange

Citrus Salad

Peel and segment citrus fruit. Halve the peeled physalis.

300ml white wine
200ml water
100g caster sugar
100ml fresh orange juice
100ml fresh grapefruit juice
100ml fresh lemon juice

Granita

Dissolve sugar in hot water, then add juices and wine.

Transfer to metal tray and freeze, stirring occasionally.

Once frozen solid, scrape with a metal spoon to create large crystals.

4 lemons with peel diced
100g caster sugar
100g glucose syrup
50ml water
50ml lemon juice
1 lemon, zested

Lemon Marmalade

Slowly cook together lemon dice, sugar, glucose syrup, water and lemon juice until mix reaches temperature of 110°C. Then add lemon zest.

Refrigerate.

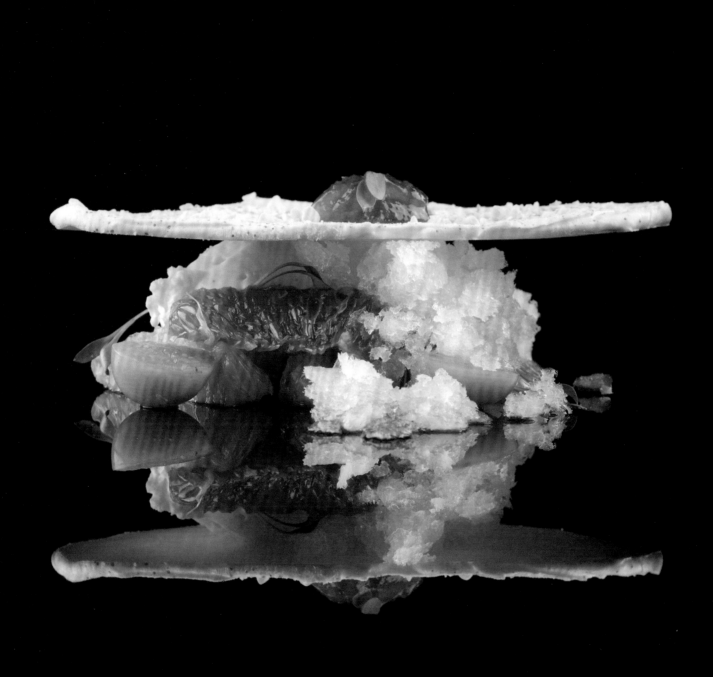

Chocolate, Pistachio and Raspberry by Neil Rankin
Serves 10

12 eggs
750g caster sugar
750g butter
700g Valrhona Tropilia 70%
125g Valrhona cocoa powder
12g baking powder
125g strong flour
300g peeled pistachios

Chocolate Brownie

Whisk eggs and sugar to a sabayon. Meanwhile, melt butter/chocolate. Sieve flour and baking powder together.

Add butter/chocolate mix to sabayon. When nearly mixed, add dry ingredients and pistachios.

Pour into lined gastronorm tray and bake in preheated oven for 17 minutes at 175ºC.

Cool at room temperature, then refrigerate/freeze to aid the cutting process.

250g bright green pistachios
Water to cover

Pistachio Paste

Simmer pistachios in water for 20-30 minutes until soft, topping up water when necessary.

Strain off water, but retain it. Blend nuts in thermomix adding water to make a smooth purée consistency.

Pass through fine strainer and chill.

750ml UHT whipping cream
250g pistachio paste
7g gelatine, soaked in cold water
150g caster sugar
200g pistachio popcorn, blended
50g Sosa raspberry crispy

Pistachio Cream

Boil half the cream with sugar, then add drained gelatine.

Mix in pistachio paste and finally remainder of the cream. Refrigerate until set firm.

Beat pistachio cream in mixer with paddle until smooth and pipeable. Pipe lengths on top of popcorn/raspberry crumb. Spoon more crumb over cream and freeze.

Cut to desired length.

100g popcorn kernels
200g caster sugar
100g pistachios, ground

Pistachio Popcorn

Pop popcorn in pan with a little oil.

In hot saucepan, make a dry caramel with sugar, then add corn and pistachio powder. Stir and turn out onto silicone paper while hot. Use a couple of forks to separate the corn.

Once cold store in airtight container.

800ml raspberry purée
200ml hot water
125g caster sugar
60g Sosa pro-sorbet

Raspberry Sorbet

Dissolve sugar in hot water, then add remainder of ingredients.

Refrigerate for 4 hours to mature the sorbet mix. Then place in pacojet beaker and freeze for minimum of 12 hours before processing.

400ml raspberry purée
100g caster sugar
1 lemon, juiced
30g Sosa vege gel

Raspberry Fluid Gel

In pan, bring all ingredients up to boil. Then remove from pan and place in fridge.

Blend in thermomix until smooth and pass through fine strainer.

Roast Pear and Tofu by Neil Rankin
Serves 10

500ml UHT whipping cream
500ml whole milk
200g egg yolks
100g caster sugar
410g Valrhona Manjari 64%

Make a crème anglaise with milk, cream, sugar and yolks making sure to reach 85°C.

Melt chocolate.

Weigh out 1kg of anglaise and add this gradually to chocolate stirring always from middle to create an elastic core and good emulsion.

Once all is incorporated blend cremeux with hand blender being careful not to incorporate any air bubbles. Refrigerate.

600ml whole milk
70g cocoa nibs
4g agar agar
25g caster sugar

Tofu

Boil milk with cocoa nibs. Remove from heat and cover with cling film to stop evaporation. Infuse for 10 minutes.

Pass through fine strainer and weigh milk again (adjust back to original weight if needed with extra milk).

Mix agar with sugar and add to milk. Bring back to boil, set in small tray 1.5cm high.

800g pear purée
200ml water
60g Sosa pro crema 100
125g caster sugar
1 lemon, juiced

Pear Sorbet

Dissolve sugar in heated water. Add rest of ingredients and mature in fridge for 4 hours.

Pour into pacojet beakers and freeze for minimum of 12 hours before processing.

500ml pear juice
100g caster sugar
1 lemon, juiced
30g Sosa vege gel

Pear Purée

Place all ingredients into saucepan and boil, stirring continuously. Pour into small tray and set.

Blend half jelly in thermomix and pass through fine strainer.

Cut other half into circles etc for garnish.

300g icing sugar
300g ground almonds
110g egg whites
110g egg whites
30g caster sugar
100ml water
300g caster sugar

Macaroons

Cut Mix almonds, icing sugar and first batch of egg whites together to form a paste.

Whisk the second batch of egg whites with 30g caster sugar on speed 6.

Boil water and second batch of caster sugar to temperature of 113°C. Then gradually pour hot sugar syrup onto meringue that is still whisking.

When the meringue is at blood temperature, mix it into the almond mix bit by bit.

Pipe mix into 3cm diameter circles and cook at 140°C for 12-14 minutes, low fan.

Refrigerate for 1 day then freeze until needed.

150g honey
280g glucose syrup
800g caster sugar
150ml water
40g bicarbonate of soda

Honeycomb

Boil honey, glucose syrup, sugar and water to light, golden caramel.

Whisk in bicarbonate of soda and pour onto a sheet of silicone paper to set. Then crush to desired size pieces.

Sabrina Gidda

Cooking and food have often gone hand in hand in many of my fondest memories. I still remember going to the floating markets in Bangkok as child, marvelling at produce I had never seen before. I remember too learning how to cook a Sunday roast at home by my mother's side.

So food, family and the memories of so many happy meals are a constant source of inspiration even today.

When I spent many of my formative academic years thinking about and planning what to eat for dinner, I grew to realise that there could be no other possible job for me.

Cooking for me is quite simply about creativity, energy and the pleasure of eating great food.

Kedgeree Scotch Egg, Curried Mayonnaise and Crispy Shallot by Sabrina Gidda
Serves 4

275g Loch Fyne smoked haddock
2 bay leaves
250g shallots
6g turmeric
4g curry powder
10g salt
8g cayenne pepper
7g parsley, finely chopped
7 eggs
100g Japanese breadcrumbs
55ml milk
10g coriander cress
30g plain flour
75ml double cream
5 black peppercorns
200g plum tomatoes
200g apricot tomatoes
75g Basmati rice
20g parsley, finely chopped
5g turmeric
1 lemon, juiced

Combine double cream, bay leaves, 100g sliced shallots, 6g turmeric, curry powder and peppercorns in saucepan and bring to boil. When cream has come to temperature, remove from heat and allow to cool before straining through muslin.

Skin and pin bone haddock. Cut into large pieces and put in food processor. Add cayenne, salt and half of the finely chopped parsley. Blend until fish has broken down into coarse mince.

Resume blending, slowly adding spice infused cream until fish and cream are mixed thoroughly. Remove and refrigerate.

Bring small saucepan of water to rapid boil, lower four room temperature eggs into pan and boil for 5½ minutes. Then cool in iced water. Carefully peel eggs and refrigerate.

Divide mousse into four and work it around boiled eggs evenly before chilling again.

Beat remaining three eggs with milk and strain through strainer. Dip each egg into flour, then egg, then Japanese breadcrumbs. Repeat again to thoroughly cover.

Cook rice until fluffy with 5g of turmeric and dress with 8g finely chopped parsley.

Quarter tomatoes, removing seeds and chop finely into neat dice. Mix with remaining parsley and lemon juice.

Finely slice remaining shallots and pop into remaining flour before frying until crisp.

Deep fry scotch egg at 170°C for 6-7 minutes, before allowing egg to rest in fryer basket above oil for further 3 minutes.

Dress dish with curried mayonnaise, coriander cress, rice and tomato salad.

Salad of Heritage Tomatoes and Laverstoke Park Mozzarella with Anchovy Vinaigrette by Sabrina Gidda
Serves 4

2 x 500g Laverstoke Park Mozzarella

400g plum tomatoes

250g baby San Marzano tomatoes

1kg Heirloom tomatoes, mixed

200g baby San Marzano yellow tomatoes

200g cherry tomatoes

200g tiger tomatoes

250ml extra virgin olive oil

150g anchovies

2 red chillies

1 lemon

15 sprigs flat leaf parsley

75ml sherry vinegar

12 cucumber flowers

25g baby basil cress

Cover baking tray with cling film and spray surface with olive oil. Slice one cherry tomato thinly and lay slices over cling film, spray again with oil and dehydrate in hot cupboard at 70°C until crisp.

Take one third of a punnet of each baby tomato and cut in half. Dress with a little olive oil and slow roast in 110°C oven until tomatoes begin to dry slightly and lose moisture.

Slice larger Heirloom tomatoes into slices, smaller tomatoes into wedges and baby tomatoes in half.

Finely chop chillies and parsley, adding sherry vinegar and virgin olive oil. Add a little lemon juice and black pepper. Lastly, add chopped anchovies.

Dress the salad by assembling mixture of raw tomato and semi dried tomato in bowl before topping with torn Mozzarella.

Garnish with vinaigrette, tomato crisps, baby basil cress and cucumber flowers.

Fillet of Turbot, Braised Fennel and Gnocchi
by Sabrina Gidda
Serves 4

4 x 175g turbot portions
50g butter
10g thyme
2 cloves garlic
130ml white wine
600ml golden chicken stock
500g large fennel
500g baby fennel
1 lemon
1 teaspoon fennel pollen
60g fennel cress
20ml good olive oil
275g Désirée potatoes
95g plain flour
Semolina flour for dusting
1 egg
250g baby San Marzano tomatoes
250g navel oranges

Cut bulb of large fennel in half to reveal its shape. Run fennel (root attached) through mandolin to create the fennel crisp.

Brush each fennel piece with olive oil, lay onto cling film lined tray and crisp in hot cupboard at 70°C.

Trim down baby fennel, setting aside fronds for garnish later. Gently warm 10ml of oil in pan before adding fennel.

Add finely chopped garlic and thyme sprigs, turning fennel carefully. Turn heat up high and add wine to deglaze pan. Allow wine to cook out before adding chicken stock.

Cover with cartouche and cook until fennel is tender but has bite. Remove fennel, increase heat once again and reduce the braising liquor by two thirds. Correct seasoning with lemon and set aside.

Boil potatoes with their skins on in salted water until they are tender. Drain and pop into oven at 150°C for 5 minutes. Peel potatoes whilst hot and rice, or pass through a moulin. Sieve in flour and salt. Begin to mix carefully by hand before adding half an egg. If mixture is a little dry, add remaining egg and work into a dough. Dust surface with semolina flour before beginning to make gnocchi.

Divide mix into four and roll out into sausage shape until dough is approximately 1.25cm in diameter. Cut into 2cm pieces and put in tray that has been well dusted with semolina flour. Refrigerate for at least half an hour.

Drizzle skin of turbot with remaining oil, making sure skin has been coated evenly. Cook fish skin side down, pressing it down to ensure even crisping. When fish has begun to cook halfway through flesh, add butter, baste and then remove from pan. Cook in oven for 4 minutes at 150°C.

Cook gnocchi in pan of boiling salted water until dumplings float to surface. In frying pan, heat drizzle of olive oil and 30g of butter. When butter is foaming, add gnocchi and cook until each dumpling has a golden crust.

Reheat fennel in braising liquor, adding fronds and fennel cress to dish as it is plated.

Segment orange, discarding any pips, sear in very hot non stick, dry pan until slightly charred.

Halve the baby San Marzano tomatoes and dress in a little house vinaigrette.

Before serving, scatter fennel pollen over dish.

Toby Stuart

Restaurants provide such a personal experience. People put their faith in us and expect us to deliver, sometimes to mark pivotal changes or great moments in their lives. So shouldn't we do everything we can to make their experience or celebration a success? This idea started to make me really think about my purpose in the restaurant.

I'm inspired day after day with the produce that comes in through our kitchen. It's impossible for me not to want to honour the life of that amazingly blue shelled native lobster, bright-eyed sea bass, perfect baby carrot or pristine lettuce leaf.

Once you see ingredients for the life that they are, do you want to waste any part of it? Destroy it by bad prep work or clumsy overcooking? I believe we have a responsibility as chefs to know where our produce comes from, how it was produced, how it was transported and how the seasons affect all of these things.

Cheese and Pickle by Toby Stuart
Serves 10

200g Dorstone goat's cheese
400ml double cream
330ml milk
1 leaf gelatine
2g salt
2g pepper

Cheese Foam
Gently warm milk with cheese. Soak gelatine in cold water.

Melt gelatine into cheese mix then add cream, salt and pepper.

Place in syphon and charge twice with two gas charges. Reserve in fridge until needed.

45ml white wine vinegar
45ml water
20g caster sugar
1 star anise
2 black peppercorns
2g gelatine
2g salt

Pickle Jelly
Place water, vinegar, sugar and spices in pan and bring to boil. Leave to infuse for 1 hour.

Soak gelatine in cold water until softened. Drain and add to spice liquid to dissolve. Leave to cool at room temperature then pass into a suitable container. Chill until required.

315g oatmeal
150g wholemeal flour
150g flour
15g sugar
10g salt
12g bicarbonate of soda
310g unsalted butter
180ml egg whites

Oat Biscuit Crumble
Mix dry ingredients in a large bowl.

Add chopped butter and mix to resemble fine breadcrumbs.

Slowly add egg whites until mixture forms a dough. Do not over mix. Refrigerate for 2 hours then roll into 2mm thick squares.

Cook at 165°C until golden (about 10 minutes).

Crumble and reserve.

50ml white wine vinegar
50g caster sugar
1 bunch baby carrots
1 bunch baby onions
1 bunch baby turnips
250g mixed salad leaves
1 bunch breakfast radish

Gastric for Vegetables
Bring vinegar and sugar to boil. Cook until syrupy, then chill.

Wash and prepare vegetables. Blanch and reserve.

Thinly slice breakfast radish on mandolin and place into iced water for 10 minutes.

Cut vegetables into bite sized pieces. Place on tray and drizzle with the gastric, good olive oil and season.

Use the radish and leaves to garnish the dish.

Quail by Toby Stuart
Serves 10

4 quail breasts
1 stick celery
1 Granny Smith apple
1 head dandelion
15g celery cress
100g Kentish cobnuts
100g quail parfait frozen
2g salt
2g pepper

Poach quail breasts in preheated waterbath at 60°C for 30 minutes.

Wash and cut large batons of apple about the size of match sticks. Dress in a little French vinaigrette.

Peel celery and baton to same size as apple.

Dress dandelions in a little French vinaigrette.

Season and roast quails in hot oil until golden. Leave to rest.

Heat sauce in a pan.

Cut each quail breast into three pieces and arrange through salad.

Sprinkle on some grated cobnuts. Pour sauce over quail.

Add shaved parfait and finish with celery cress.

4 quail carcasses
50g unsalted butter
40g shallots
30g carrots
30g leeks
10 cloves garlic
10g thyme
10 bay leaves
10g white peppercorns
100ml brandy
150ml white wine
150ml Maderia
1ltr brown chicken stock

Quail Sauce

Chop quail carcasses into several pieces then caramelize in hot oil until deep brown. Add washed and trimmed vegetables and garlic to same pan, and colour. Add herbs and peppercorns.

Strain off fat.

Deglaze with brandy. Add white wine and Madeira.

Reduce to syrup. Add stock and simmer for 2 hours.

Adjust seasoning, pour through fine strainer and reserve until needed.

50g quail livers
50g chicken livers
100g unsalted butter
40g shallots
3 cloves garlic
20g thyme
1 egg
50ml brandy
50ml port

Quail Liver Parfait

Finely chop shallots and garlic. Sweat with thyme leaves in a little olive oil.

Add port and brandy and reduce to syrup.

Allow egg and livers to reach room temperature. Melt butter.

Blend livers with the reduction, drop in egg and finally pour in butter, melted and warm.

Pass through fine strainer and pour into suitable mould. Cover with foil and cook at 130°C for 30 minutes until set.

Leave to cool at room temperature. Refrigerate and freeze.

To serve, shave into thin slices on a mandolin or slicer.

Collar of Gloucester Old Spot Pork by Toby Stuart
Serves 10

1kg pork fat trim	**Pork Collar**
200ml water	Rub the pork with a little olive oil then place into a vacuum pack bag and seal on full pressure. Cook in waterbath set to 65°C for 24 hours and then chill.
	Remove from bag and seal in a hot pan butter, season and roast until caramelised and hot in the centre.

Pork Collar

1kg pork fat trim
200ml water

Rub the pork with a little olive oil then place into a vacuum pack bag and seal on full pressure. Cook in waterbath set to 65°C for 24 hours and then chill.

Remove from bag and seal in a hot pan butter, season and roast until caramelised and hot in the centre.

1kg pork trimmings
100g pork fat
2 cloves garlic, whole
¼ bunch of thyme
20g tomato purée
2 plum tomatoes, quartered
1 white onion, finely sliced
350ml dry white wine
2 sprigs flat leaf parsley
1ltr basic veal stock
Water

Roasted Pork Fat

Preheat oven to 120°C. Place fat into heavy bottomed saucepan. Add the water.

Cover with foil and cook in low oven for about 4 hours, or until all water has evaporated and the fat is starting to colour. It should be a slight golden brown colour with the aroma of roast pork.

Strain and leave to cool. Refrigerate.

6 onions
2 garlic cloves
50g butter
100ml double cream
1 sprig of thyme
Salt, pepper and sugar to taste

Pork Sauce

In heavy based saucepan, colour pork trimmings and pork fat. Add garlic, thyme, tomato purée, plum tomatoes and onion. Cook out for 1 minute.

Add wine and parsley. Cover using 70% veal stock and 30% water. Bring to boil, skim and reduce heat. Simmer for 1 hour.

Infuse for 1 hour. Pass through fine strainer and reduce until correct consistency has been achieved.

Just before serving split sauce with a little roasted pork fat.

400g Granny Smith apples	**Onion Purée**
30g butter	Peel and dice onions. Sweat onions and garlic cloves in butter very slowly in heavy based saucepan with tight fitting lid for 5-10 minutes, until transparent but not coloured.
Salt	
½ lemon, juiced	
30ml water	

Onion Purée

Peel and dice onions. Sweat onions and garlic cloves in butter very slowly in heavy based saucepan with tight fitting lid for 5-10 minutes, until transparent but not coloured.

Add thyme and seasoning. Cover with tight fitting lid and cook in slow oven at 150-170°C for 20-30 minutes (no colour at all).

Remove thyme and purée onion until smooth. Pass through fine strainer.

Bring cream to boil and add gradually to purée until very smooth.

Correct seasoning and reserve until needed.

400g Granny Smith apples
30g butter
Salt
½ lemon, juiced
30ml water

70g sage, roughly chopped
1ltr grapeseed oil
10g salt

Apple Compote

Peel apples into acidulated water. Dice apples into 2cm cubes, keeping the trimmings. Blanch in boiling water for 10 seconds. Refresh in iced water, then drain.

Place water, butter and apple trimmings into pan. Cover with lid and bring to simmer. Cook until very soft and smooth.

Leave to cool and fold in apple dice creating a thick chutney like consistency.

Reserve.

250ml sage oil
20g parsley, blanched
1 egg
20ml white wine vinegar
Seasoning

Sage Oil

Place sage, oil and salt into vacuum pack bag. Cook at 62°C for 30 minutes in waterbath.

Refrigerate in bag and strain once cooled.

Sage Emulsion

Cook egg in its shell for 7 minutes.

Place cooked parsley, egg and vinegar into blender and blend until smooth. Trickle in sage oil until thick mayonnaise has been achieved.

Place into sauce bottle and serve.

400g potatoes
4 cloves garlic
6 sprigs thyme
40ml olive oil
50g butter
3g salt

Parisienne Potatoes

Using a parisienne scoop, make even sized balls from potatoes.

Season and roast in a little oil with cloves of garlic and sprigs of thyme. Once coloured, add some butter and place into medium heat oven turning regularly until cooked and soft. Season with salt to taste.

Des Artiss

Cooking is such a large part of my life. Food is
so important, and we're truly fortunate to work
with some of very best produce available when so
many people do not have enough to eat.

Cooking has taken me all over the world, to places
as far apart as Kazakhstan, France and Suffolk. But
the British Isles are still my great love. There's
such a multitude of amazing places to eat here. I
draw my inspiration from the great people I work
with and from local food producers. In the work
that we do you have to keep striving every day to
achieve.

As someone quite close to me once said, 'cooking
is about bringing people together'.

Langoustine by Des Artiss
Serves 10

10 langoustines
100g sea purslane
1 bunch sea beet
100g samphire
50g butter
750ml bisque sauce

1kg 00 flour
9 eggs
40ml olive oil
1g salt

2.5kg langoustines
400ml double cream
3 eggs
10g salt
5g pepper

1kg crab shells
200g leeks
200g onions
200g carrots
1 head garlic
1 bottle white wine
250ml brandy
40g thyme
1kg trimmed flat fish bones
500g fennel
60g tomato purée
1ltr double cream
28g butter
2ltr water

Pasta

Place flour in food processor with egg yolks, olive oil and salt. Blend to a light breadcrumb looking mixture.

Turn out onto lightly floured surface and knead for 10 minutes until mix has stiffened.

Vacuum pack tightly and refrigerate for 1 hour.

Langoustine Mousse

Peel and de-vein langoustines. Blast chill for 10 minutes until really cold. Keep ten langoustines aside for ravioli.

Place in blender with two egg whites and salt. Blend until smooth.

Pass through drum sieve and chill again. Weigh purée.

Beat in equal weight of double cream.

Check seasoning, wrap a little mousse in cling film and poach gently until set in order to test consistency. It should be set but not bouncy and too firm. If it is then beat in a little more cream.

Set aside in fridge.

Roll out pasta dough and make raviolis using beaten egg yolk to seal. Place one langoustine tail in each ravioli with mousse.

Place on tray dusted with semolina or use silicone paper.

Blanch and keep warm.

Bisque Sauce

Roast shells until golden in oven.

Peel, wash and trim vegetables. Lightly brown in a pan with butter.

In larger pan, sweat fish bones, add crab bones and break them down using rolling pin for more surface area.

Add vegetables and brandy and bring to boil. Light with a match and flame.

Add white wine and reduce to a glaze. Add thyme, garlic, tomato purée and top up with water.

Simmer gently and skim regularly. Cook for at least 2 hours until it has reduced by half.

Strain stock through muslin and reduce to 500ml.

Add double cream and reduce to a light sauce consistency. Season and keep warm.

To serve

Cook raviolis, dress with a little olive oil then cover and keep warm.

Pick and wash sea beet, then wilt it in a little butter. Season and keep warm.

Pick, wash and blanch samphire in salted water. Dress with butter and keep warm.

Pick, wash and blanch purslane. Dress with butter and keep warm.

Arrange sea beet and ravioli in a bowl.

Aerate bisque sauce with a hand mixer, and dress.

Garnish with sea herbs and vegetables.

Galloway Beef by Des Artiss
Serves 10

10 x 150g Galloway beef fillets
Artichoke purée
10 fondant potatoes
200ml jus
250g baby spinach
50g butter
250g girolles mushrooms
20g horseradish root
½ bunch flat leaf parsley

2kg large red waxy potatoes
1 head of garlic
40g thyme
325g butter
2g salt

600g Jerusalem artichokes
120g butter
100ml semi skimmed milk
500ml double cream
2g salt
2g pepper

Fondant Potatoes

Trim potatoes and cut out using a cylindrical fondant cutter.

Melt butter, add thyme and season. Cut head of garlic in half and add to appropriate sized pan, then add potatoes. Place over low to medium heat, allow butter to foam up around potatoes and colour on one side.

When lightly golden, remove from heat and allow to cool.

Turn potatoes over and place back on low to medium heat and repeat process. The foaming butter should cook potatoes through to middle.

Set aside and keep warm.

Artichoke Purée

Peel artichokes into lemon water. Cut into even sized pieces.

Melt butter and sweat artichokes until opaque.

Add milk and cream. Simmer gently until it starts to thicken and artichokes are cooked through and very soft.

Blend until smooth, then pass through a fine sieve.

Check seasoning, place in pan and cover with cling film to prevent from skinning.

Set aside and keep warm.

To serve

Season and seal beef, add butter and foam. Cook until core temperature is reached. Rest.

Heat artichoke purée, cover with cling film and set aside until needed.

Wash, dry and prepare girolles. Pan fry in a little butter. When coloured, add a dessert spoon of water to make an emulsion and finish cooking. Drain and keep warm.

Pick over, wash and dry spinach. Season and wilt in a little butter. Drain and keep warm.

Warm fondants, drain and keep warm.

Chop parsley, grate horseradish on microplane. Heat jus, add horseradish and parsley.

Arrange ingredients on plate and dress with jus.

Jason Atherton

Cooking saved my life its as simple as that.
As a small boy I never dreamed of being a
footballer or anything like that, well maybe
being part of take that!

Then I found food or food found me as it
never entered into my head I would one
day become a michlien starred chef. I just
totally fell in love with food , kitchens
and restaurants and would carry a note
pad to work and draw my perfect kitchen
and restaurant. I owe my whole life to the
beautiful art of being a chef and I wouldn't
change it for the world. Food has consumed my
life and is with me everywhere I go.

Scallop Ceviche by Jason Atherton
Serves 4

12 hand dived scallops
1 cucumber
100ml dressing
5g salt
1 lemon
6 breakfast radishes
1 Granny Smith apple
1 mouli
25g sea herbs

225ml soy sauce
150ml mirin
75ml vegetable oil
75ml rice vinegar
75g clear honey
1g pepper
40g wasabi paste
1g mustard seeds
50ml yuzu

250ml buttermilk
250g horseradish
550ml milk
550ml double cream
20g corn starch

Remove scallops from the shell and clean well. Drain and pat dry. Freeze scallops for 12 hours and then allow to defrost in fridge.

Peel cucumber and place into vacuum pack bag. Seal on full vacuum and leave until cucumber turns translucent.

Finely slice radishes 1mm thick on Japanese mandolin and place into iced water.

Peel Granny Smith apples and cut into fine batons.

Season scallops with salt and then spoon over dressing until completely covered. Leave for 5-6 minutes. Pour off excess dressing.

Slice cucumber into 5mm thick slices and arrange with scallops on the plate. Dress with the apple, radish and finally grate on the horseradish 'snow' using a microplane grater.

Dressing
Blend wasabi and soy sauce, then whisk in rest of ingredients.

Horseradish Snow
Peel and juice horseradish in juicer, reserving liquid.

Combine milk and cream and heat. Thicken with corn starch. Add buttermilk, horseradish juice and season. Cool.

Pour into pacojet beakers and freeze to -18°C.

Blitz a little at a time and scrape into container. Refreeze until required.

Cornish Sea Bass and Celeriac by Jason Atherton
Serves 4

4 Cornish sea bass fillets

Sea Bass

Ensure fillets are clean, pin boned and free from scales.

Trim into neat fillets, removing any excess fatty belly.

Season with salt then pan fry in a little oil until lightly golden brown and just cooked through.

1 celeriac
60g rock salt

Salt Baked Celeriac

Scrub and wrap whole celeriac in foil with rock salt.

Bake at 160°C for 5-6 hours until soft. Leave to cool.

Cut into 15mm thick slices, then cut out with a 40mm fondant cutter.

3 sticks celery
100g crosnes

Cut the left over pieces into rough shapes for roasting.

1 celeriac
70g butter
700ml milk
2g salt
2g pepper

Celery Batons

Peel and cut celery into 10cm batons. Blanch in seasoned water. Refresh and reserve.

Blanch crosnes in seasoned water and refresh.

200g potatoes
200g celeriac

Celeriac Purée

Scrub and clean celeriac and remove all roots. Dice, keeping skin on.

Place in pan with butter and milk. Bring to boil and simmer until tender.

2kg celeriac
500g carrots
500g celery
500g shallots
3 cloves garlic
30g thyme
100g tomato purée
500ml red wine
20ml truffle oil
20ml truffle juice
40g ultratex

Place in thermomix and blend to a smooth purée. Correct seasoning.

Celeriac Cous Cous

In thermomix blitz peeled potato and peeled celeriac with 200ml water to sand like texture.

Place in strainer and wash all starch off. Pat dry and spread on tray to dry out.

Shallow fry until golden. Drain on kitchen paper and season.

Celeriac Truffle Sauce

Scrub and clean celeriac. Dice and roast until dark in colour. Place in pan of water, just enough to cover, and leave to steep.

Peel carrots, celery and shallots and cut into rough pieces. Place in roasting pan and roast in hot oven with thyme and garlic.

Add tomato purée to vegetables and cook out slowly, mixing well.

Add wine and reduce until all has evaporated.

Once water has infused, add this and celeriac to pan. Reduce by half and pass through fine strainer.

Add truffle oil and truffle jus. Thicken with ultratex.

Peanut Butter and Cherry Jam Sandwich by Jason Atherton
Serves 4

150g caster sugar
240ml egg whites
3tbls water

Italian Meringue

Whisk egg whites to soft peak stage. Combine sugar with water and boil until it reaches 120°C.

Trickle syrup into egg whites, whisking on slow speed.

Continue whisking until cold, firm and glossy.

450g sweet peanut butter
1050ml double cream
135ml Frangelico
300g caster sugar
6 eggs
120ml egg yolks

Peanut Parfait

Make a pâté à bombe with sugar, eggs and egg yolks.

Whilst pâté à bombe is whisking, make paste with peanut butter, 300ml cream and Frangelico.

When pâté à bombe has cooled whisk into peanut paste. Semi whip 750ml cream and fold into mix.

Fold in the Italian meringue. Freeze into container until required.

1ltr cherry purée
250g caster sugar
18g pectin x58

Cherry Jam

Mix pectin and sugar together.

Bring cherry purée to boil. Whilst whisking, gradually pour in pectin mix. Boil for 10 minutes, stirring occasionally.

Pass through fine strainer then cool and blend to smooth purée.

1kg butter
400ml double cream
1.2kg sugar
24g pectin x58
1.4kg flaked almonds
400g liquid glucose

Bricelet Mix

Mix together sugar and pectin.

Put pectin mix, cream, glucose and butter in pan. Bring to 95°C and stir continuously.

Pulse almonds in food processor to chop. Add almonds to the mix and stir well.

Pour onto baking tray 2.5cm high and bake at 160°C for 4 minutes.

500g cherry purée
40g caster sugar
5g citric acid
40g Sosa prospuma 100

Cherry Sorbet

Place all ingredients together and mix well. Leave in fridge for 2 hours then blend for 1 minute.

Pour into pacojet beaker and freeze until solid. When needed process in pacojet.

Albert Roux, OBE

Cooking for me is giving joy to a
multitude of people. I have a strong
belief that food unites people. The French
have always been very good at doing this -
whether it's a family reunion, a political
event or a business meeting. They always
seem to come to a happy ending around a
good plate of food and a glass of wine.

Good food doesn't need to be expensive. A
well done omelette with a nice salad and
a glass of wine is as enjoyable as a filet
of beef. I was born during the war when
food was very scarce and my mother had to
make ends meet. Lunch on Friday was wafers
with her homemade pear preserve - and what
a delicious lunch. Wednesday was risotto,
chicken feet, neck of the chicken,
gizzards, lung and heart. Again the memory
of this taste is so vivid in my mind. The
aroma as I went up the staircase made me
climb even faster. I was anxious to get
stuck in.

Lobster Mousseline and Caviar by Albert Roux OBE
Serves 10

2 medium lobsters
1 large lobster
30g salt
60ml egg white
750ml double cream
150g spinach
50g Beluga caviar
2g salt

150g shallots
200ml champagne
300g unsalted butter
50g lobster roe

Humanely kill lobsters. Remove lobster roe and reserve. Bring pan of water to boil. Rinse lobsters in cold water and plunge the two medium ones into water for 12 minutes. Remove and cool.

Remove meat from shells and slice medallions from tail. Dice remaining meat and keep in a bowl.

Take large lobster, then crack claws and take out meat. Cut open tail and remove meat. Discard gritty sac from near coral in head.

Put meat (about 400g) into food processor and blend with egg white and salt. Rub through sieve into clean bowl set over ice. Slowly add double cream. The mix should be soft and slightly runny. Chill in fridge.

Bring pan of seasoned water to boil. Remove stalks from spinach and blanch for 30 seconds. Refresh, drain and dry out on cloth.

Preheat oven to 200°C, brush sides of dariole moulds with melted butter and line with spinach leaves. Half fill with lobster mousse. Spoon in small amount of caviar and top up with mousse. Cover mousse with spinach leaves.

Place dariole moulds in bain-marie and pour hot water into bain-marie around the moulds. Cover with foil and bake for 18 minutes at 160°C.

Beurre Blanc

Peel and finely chop shallots. Place in pan with champagne and reduce until syrupy.

Take pan off heat and beat in a little of the butter. Set over low heat and slowly add remaining butter.

When butter becomes creamy add crushed lobster eggs. Correct seasoning.

To Serve

Wrap lobster medallions in foil and place in low oven (140°C) to warm through.

De-mould lobster mousselines carefully and top each one with a lobster medallion and a little caviar.

Pass beurre blanc through fine sieve and spoon around mousseline.

Pigenneaux aux Petit Pois et Herbillettes
by Albert Roux OBE
Serves 4

1 baby gem lettuce
1kg fresh peas
30g unsalted butter
5g sugar
100g ham

Lettuce and Peas

Quarter lettuce and wash in cold water. Drain and shred.

Shell peas and rinse in cold water.

Place butter and lettuce in casserole and sweat for 1 minute. Add peas and sugar. Cover and simmer for 2-3 minutes. Add ham and keep warm until needed.

4 Bresse pigeons
30g basil
30g chives
30g parsley
40ml groundnut oil
2 cloves garlic
200g shallots
200g carrots
20g thyme
6g salt
2g pepper

Pigeon

Season cavities with salt and pepper and put a spoonful of fresh herbs into each one.

Heat oil and garlic cloves in roasting pan, add pigeon trimmings and giblets. Add pigeons and brown all sides. Add sliced shallots, peeled and sliced carrots and thyme sprigs. Cook in preheated oven at 180°C for 14 minutes.

Lay breast side down on serving plate and cover until needed.

Add garlic cloves to lettuce and peas.

150ml chicken stock
2g salt
2g pepper

The Sauce

Pour off half cooking fat from roasting pan and deglaze with chicken stock.

Strain sauce through strainer, season with salt and pepper.

60g watercress

To Serve

Split pigeon breasts and lay them on bed of peas and lettuce.

Garnish with watercress. Spoon over sauce.

Sablé aux Fraises by Albert Roux OBE
Serves 6

Sablé Biscuit

200g unsalted butter
2g salt
100g icing sugar
60ml egg yolks
250g plain flour
2 eggs

Cut butter into small pieces and work until soft with your fingertips. Sift icing sugar and salt onto butter and mix well.

Add egg yolks and lightly mix until incorporated. Sift in flour and slowly work into smooth dough. Rub a couple of times to mix.

Roll into ball and flatten. Refrigerate for several hours.

800g strawberries
250ml simple sugar syrup
1 lemon

Preheat oven to 200°C, roll out pastry to thickness of 2mm and cut out 18 circles with a 10cm cutter. Brush 6 of the circles with egg wash.

Bake circles for about 8 minutes. Cool and transfer to wire rack.

800g strawberries

Strawberry Coulis

Hull, wash and drain strawberries. Purée in blender with syrup and lemon juice.

Rub through fine strainer to extract as much juice as possible.

Refrigerate until needed.

Strawberries

Wash and hull strawberries, halving them if necessary.

Roll in two thirds of coulis and set aside in fridge until needed.

To Serve

Place an unglazed shortbread circle on plate. Spread over few strawberries and place a second second shortbread circle on top. Add another layer of strawberries and top with a glazed shortbread.

Serve with strawberry coulis.

Concept and design by FRASERS.eu.com
Photography by Mark Suddaby